FEBRUARY

M	T	W	T	F	S	S
			1	2	3	4
5	6	7	8	9	10	11
12	13	14	15	16	17	18
19	20	21	22	23	24	25
26	27	28	29			

APRIL

M	T	W	T	F	S	S
1	2	3	4	5	6	7
8	9	10	11	12	13	14
15	16	17	18	19	20	21
22	23	24	25	26	27	28
29	30					

JUNE

M	T	W	T	F	S	S
					1	2
3	4	5	6	7	8	9
10	11	12	13	14	15	16
17	18	19	20	21	22	23
24	25	26	27	28	29	30

THE
ALMANAC

THE
ALMANAC

A SEASONAL GUIDE TO
2024

LIA LEENDERTZ

With illustrations by Aitch

First published in Great Britain in 2023 by Gaia, an imprint of
Octopus Publishing Group Ltd
Carmelite House
50 Victoria Embankment
London EC4Y 0DZ
www.octopusbooks.co.uk

An Hachette UK Company
www.hachette.co.uk

ISBN 978-1-85675-464-4

A CIP catalogue record for this book is available from the British Library.

Printed and bound in the United Kingdom.

10 9 8 7 6 5 4 3 2 1

Publisher: Stephanie Jackson
Creative Director: Jonathan Christie
Designer: Matt Cox at Newman+Eastwood
Senior Editor: Pauline Bache
Copy Editors: Alison Wormleighton and Laura Gladwin
Senior Production Manager: Peter Hunt

This FSC® label means that materials used for the product have been
responsibly sourced

Ovens should be preheated to the specific temperature – for fan-assisted ovens,
follow manufacturer's instructions for adjusting the time and the temperature.
All efforts have been made to ensure the dates within this almanac are correct,
but some may be subject to cancellation or rearrangement after publication.

CONTENTS

INTRODUCTION

Welcome to *The Almanac: A Seasonal Guide to 2024*! Hello to new readers – I hope you enjoy your first year with the almanac by your side. And welcome back to regular readers – thank you for making my almanacs a part of your annual traditions.

My aim every year is to fill this book with keys for unlocking the magic of every month, to help you mark and celebrate the unfolding of each season. It is so easy to let the year fly by and not notice what is special about a particular time, especially as the changes may be so gradual that you don't notice them. With this almanac by your side you will find new ways of marking the year along with ideas and inspiration for getting the most from each season – I hope you are tempted to take up some of them.

The Almanac's theme this year is the garden, from the first stirrings of green buds in spring to the falling of leaves and on to winter when much of nature hibernates. We have monthly garden and weather folklore; garden crafts; misty-eyed folk songs set in flower-filled gardens; gardening by the moon; the goings-on of the creatures that make homes in our borders and hedges; and a guide to the best pollen-rich flowers for every season.

And, of course, we have our regulars, including each month's festivals and other important dates; moon phases, sunrises and sunsets; the timing of every high tide and spring tide; the procession of planets that pass over in the ssky at night, and all the supermoons, meteor showers and eclipses to be aware of this year. Plus, for something a little different this year, the wonderful and wise Louise Press joins us with guidance and meditations based on the full moon and new moon energies of the month.

Finally, as ever, I have included seasonal and celebratory recipes, with a 'snack of the month' this year – something irresistible, salty and crunchy to enjoy, perhaps with a refreshing drink after one of those long days in the garden.

Now, over to you to enjoy many magical moments marking the natural rhythms of the year ahead. Have a wonderful 2024.

Lia Leendertz

Lia Leendertz

THE YEAR AHEAD

The year

Gregorian year	2024, begins 1st January
Japanese year	2684, begins 1st January
Chinese year	Green Wood Dragon, begins 10th February
Islamic year	1446, begins 7th July
Coptic year	1741, begins 11th September
Jewish year	5785, begins 2nd October

The sky at night in the year ahead

This is unfortunately not going to be a vintage year for spotting the bright planets, simply because most of them will spend several months hidden in the glare of the sun.

Venus starts 2024 as a bright morning star visible for about two hours before sunrise, but by mid-February it will be lost in the glare of the sun. It will remain difficult to see until the end of November and by year's end will be a bright evening star.

Mars will be difficult to see for the first half of the year as it will be dim and close to the sun. By July it will be visible as a morning star in the east an hour or so before sunrise. By the end of the year, it will be high and bright all night.

Jupiter starts the year high and bright after sunset. By mid-March it will become an evening star and by May it will be lost in the dusk. By July it will have reappeared as a morning star shortly before sunrise. From then on it will rise earlier each day until the end of the year, being at its highest and brightest around midnight at the beginning of December.

Saturn will be difficult to see this year. Saturn's rings will be nearly edge-on and so it will not appear bright. It will be several years before the rings open out to make Saturn really shine. This year the best time for viewing it will be September, around midnight, at an altitude of 30 degrees in the south.

There will be two eclipses of the sun, as there are in most years, one in spring and one in autumn. Unfortunately, they will not be visible from the UK since they will occur beneath the horizon. There will also be two lunar eclipses, a penumbral one in spring and a partial lunar eclipse in autumn.

The Quadrantid meteor shower in January and the Perseid

meteor shower in August will have dark skies some of the time, but the full moon will detract from the Geminid meteor shower in December.

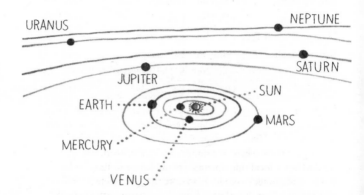

The position of the planets of the solar system on 1st January 2024

Notes on using the tide times

The full tide timetable given each month is <u>for Dover</u>, because Dover is widely used as a standard port from which to work out all other tide times. Every port has a 'high water time difference on Dover' figure, which you can find on the internet. For instance, Bristol's high water time difference on Dover is −4h 10m, and so, looking at this almanac's visual tide timetable, you would just trace your finger back along it 4 hours and 10 minutes to see that a midday high tide at Dover would mean it will be high tide at Bristol at 07.50. London Bridge's is +2h 52m, so – tracing forwards – a midday high tide at Dover would see a high tide in London at 14.52. Once you know any local port's figure, you can just trace that amount of time backwards or forwards along the Dover tideline.

Here are a few high water time differences on Dover. Find others online by searching 'high water time difference on Dover'.

Aberdeen	+2h 31m	Bristol	−4h 10m
Firth of Forth	+3h 50m	London Bridge	+2h 52m
Port Glasgow	+1h 32m	Cowes	+0h 29m
Newcastle upon Tyne	+4h 33m	Lyme Regis	−4h 55m
Belfast Lough	+0h 7m	Newquay	−6h 4m
Hull	−4h 52m	St Helier, Jersey	−4h 55m
Liverpool	+0h 14m	Galway Bay	−5h 55m
Cork	−5h 23m	Carlingford Lough	+0h 35m
Swansea	−4h 50m	Holyhead	−0h 50m

Do not use these where accuracy is critical; instead, you will need to buy a local tide timetable or subscribe to Easy Tide, www.ukho.gov.uk/easytide. Also note that no timetable will take into account the effects of wind and barometric pressure.

Spring and neap tide dates are also included. Spring tides are the the highest and lowest tides of the month and neap tides are the least extreme. Spring tides are a result of the pull that occurs when the sun, moon and earth are aligned. Alignment occurs at new moon and full moon, but the surge – the spring tide – is slightly delayed (usually one to three days) because of the mass of water. If you are a keen rock-pooler, beachcomber or mudlark, a low spring tide will bring the best revelations.

General notes

All times in this almanac have been adjusted for British Summer Time/Irish Standard Time, when relevant.

Coton in the Elms in Derbyshire has been chosen for the sunrise and sunset times because it has a claim as the furthest place in the UK from coastal waters, at 113 kilometres from the sea.

On the sunrise and sunset tables, black represents night, grey twilight, and white day.

January

1 New Year's Day – bank holiday in England, Wales, Scotland, Northern Ireland, Ireland

2 Bank holiday, Scotland

5 Twelfth Night (Christian/traditional)

6 Epiphany/Three Kings' Day/Little Christmas (Christian)

6 Nollaig na mBan/Women's Christmas (Christian/Irish traditional)

7 Orthodox Christmas Day (Orthodox Christian)

8 Plough Monday (English traditional)

13 Lohri (Punjabi winter festival)

17 Old Twelfth Night (traditional)

25 Burns Night (Scottish traditional)

26 26th–28th: RSPB Big Garden Birdwatch

JANUARY IN THE GARDEN

In the January garden the rich, cold earth is glazed with a bloom of frost. Containers that gathered sulky pools of water earlier in winter have turned magical: distressed and ancient looking glasses, some of them shattered into jagged shards.

The cold-forced neglect is evident everywhere – while we were baking mince pies and watching telly with tricky relatives, the weeds have taken advantage of us, at least during the milder spells, and have slunk slow but unchallenged across the cool earth. Crab apples lie where they fell, softened and browning on the lawn. Leaves have gathered sullenly around shrubs, like skirts, and in the corners of patios, the glorious golds, reds and ambers of autumn just a memory. All the leaves have turned to dull sludgy brown by the great leveller that is winter rain. They are well along their path to returning to the earth now: next stop rich, loamy compost.

The winter sun, falling in shafts between the deep shadows of the buildings, does not reach nearly high enough in the sky to clear the rooftops. And in one of those slices of weak sun a gardener might work, feeling the faint warmth of it through their jacket, producing a golden cloud with each breath out, doing the slow tasks that create the framework for the year ahead. They cut the apple wood while it sleeps, curtailing and directing future growth, picturing the year's stems and where they might be led. The eyes see bare twigs but the mind sees spring blossom, rain falling on summer leaves, the ripening apples of autumn blushed with red.

The gardener is not the only sign that the year is turning towards the light. Bulb shoots spear up through the earth, new-year green among the world-weary evergreens. Hazel catkins make clean, vertical, green-gold stripes among the tangled growth, taking their chance to spread windblown pollen while the way is clear of pesky leaves. And then, towards the end of the month, like a traveller from another time, there is a single primrose, living up to its name's likely Latin origin – *prima rosa*, meaning the 'first rose', or flower.

Garden and weather folklore

January has long been considered a month that holds prophecies for the year ahead, and this is reflected in several bits of January weather lore in which particular days are supposed to set the tone for the whole year's weather.

The feast day of St Vincent of Saragossa, patron saint of vintners and vinegar makers, on the 22nd January is one such day:

> 'Remember on St Vincent's Day, if the sun his beams display,
> 'tis a token bright and clear, of prosperous weather all the
> year.'

If that fails, we can pin our hopes on St Paul the Apostle's Day, on the 25th. Great store was apparently once set on it, not only for forecasts of the year's weather and its corresponding effect on the price of grain, but for darker prognostications:

> 'If St Paul's day be fair and clear, it does betide a happy year
> But if it chance to snow or rain, then will be dear all kind
> of grain
> If clouds or mists do dark the sky, great store of birds and
> beasts shall die
> And if the winds do fly aloft, then war shall vex the
> kingdom oft.'

This approach has much in common with *las cabañuelas*, a method of weather forecasting that originated in Spain and is still found throughout the Hispanic world. The weather on each of the first 12 days of January represents the weather of the 12 months of the year – the 1st represents January, the 2nd February and so on. From the 13th to the 24th day this is repeated, but running backwards. The final days are split up and the same done again, and then the 31st is divided into 12 parts and measurements taken of each. All of this is collated to create a weather forecast for the year.

THE SEA

Average sea temperature in Celcius

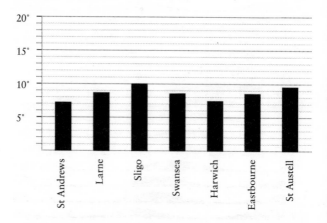

Spring and neap tides

Spring tides are the most extreme tides of the month, with the highest rises and the lowest falls, and they follow a couple of days after the full moon and new moon. These are the times to choose a low tide and go rock-pooling, mudlarking or coastal fossil-hunting. Neap tides are the least extreme, with the smallest movement, and they fall in between the spring tides.

Spring tides: 12th–14th and 26th–28th

Neap tides: 4th–6th and 18th–20th

Spring tides are shaded in black in the chart opposite.

January tide timetable for Dover

For guidance on how to convert this for your local area, see page 8.

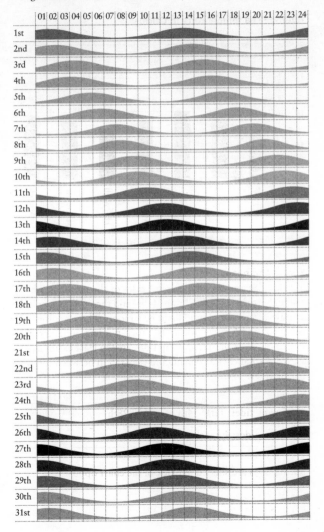

THE SKY

Stars, meteor showers and planets

At the start of the month look out for Venus in the mornings – it will rise at 05.30 in the southeast and be visible for about two hours. Mars will be too close to the sun to be seen this month. Jupiter will become visible in the dusk around 17.00 high in the southern sky. Saturn will become visible low in the southwest at about the same time. It starts the year as an evening star and will then be lost in the glare of the sun for several months. Unfortunately, it will be dim for the whole year because we will be viewing the rings almost edge-on.

3rd–4th: Quadrantid meteor shower. The best time for viewing will be from about 19.00 on the 3rd until 06.00 on the 4th. A half-moon will rise around midnight, obscuring the fainter trails.
14th: Close approach of the moon and Saturn. They will first appear in the dusk in the southwest at around 17.00 at an altitude of 22 degrees. They will set in the west at about 19.40.
18th: Close approach of the moon and Jupiter. They will appear in the dusk in the southeast at around 17.00 at around 48 degrees altitude. They will set at 01.20 the next day.

The sun

3rd: Perihelion. This is the moment in the year when the earth is nearest the sun in its imperfect elliptical orbit. At 00.38 the sun will be 147,100,632 kilometres away (compare with aphelion on 5th July, page 152).
21st: At solar noon the sun will reach an altitude of 18 degrees in the London sky and 14 degrees in the Glasgow sky.

Sunrise and set
Coton in the Elms, Derbyshire

Moonrise and set

Like the sun, the moon rises roughly in the east and sets roughly in the west. It also rises around 50 minutes later each day. Use the following guide to work out approximate moonrise times.

Full moon: Rises near sunset, opposite the sun, so in the east as the sun sets in the west.
Last quarter: Rises around midnight, and is at its highest point as the sun rises.
New moon: Rises at sunrise, in the same part of the sky as the sun, and so cannot be seen.
First quarter: Rises near noon, and is at its highest point as the sun sets.

Moon phases

Last quarter – 4th January, 03.30

New moon – 11th January, 11.57

First quarter – 18th January, 03.53

Full moon – 25th January, 17.54

The times given above are for the exact moment each moon phase occurs, for instance the moment that the moon is at its fullest.

January's full moon is known as the Wolf Moon or Stay at Home Moon.

Moon phases for January

1st	2nd	3rd	4th	5th

6th	7th	8th	9th	10th

11th NEW	12th	13th	14th	15th

16th	17th	18th	19th	20th

21st	22nd	23rd	24th	25th FULL

26th	27th	28th	29th	30th

31st				

MEDITATIONS

January's influences and guidance from Louise Press

This midwinter month is perfect for dreaming into the coming year. The darkness invites us back home to ourselves, drawing us inwards, removing the protective layers we have built up over the past year. January exposes us, lays us bare like the oak tree. We are at our most intuitive at this time of the year – there is a clarity to January like you'll find in no other month. All is quiet, all is still. It is time to do our inner work. The busyness of the festive season is behind us; we can take in a deep breath and give out a long sigh, releasing tension in our body and creating spaciousness from which to dive deeply into this transformational month.

Contrary to popular belief, January is not the time for new beginnings – it is time for rest, reflection and imaginings. It's time for contemplation, for daring to believe in our wildest dreams. January is an invitation to consider a new way of being. It gifts us with time to plan and explore possibilities for the coming year. Our dreams and intentions at the beginning of any cycle set the scene for the journey ahead. Remember…energy flows where attention goes. Imagine your 2024 story as if it were already written.

The lunar cycle can help guide our decisions and actions during the year ahead. This month the new moon will be rising on the 11th in the astrological sign of Capricorn. Echoing the seasonal energies, it heralds the time for forethought and planning. Capricorn encourages us to focus on our purpose and manifest our practical magic. This new moon will help ground our dreams by giving them roots from which to grow productively and efficiently. As we approach the end of the month, our moon blossoms full on the 25th in the bold and courageous sign of Leo. This is the time to express our truth. However, we're still doing the inner work and dreaming of our plans for the year ahead, so we can use the illumination of this full moon to strengthen and protect our energy in preparation to stride boldly forth into 2024.

Making a space for January

Every month in this almanac I am going to encourage you to make a space indoors that marks out the change from one month to the next, where you can bring the outdoors in, and perhaps take a quiet moment to think about the changing season and your place in it.

Choose a space and clear it. If you want to use it for quiet moments and meditation, select a quiet, tucked-away spot, perhaps even a cupboard or a box that you can close. If you want everyone to see it and contribute to it – and, of course, admire it – as they come and go, make it on a hall or kitchen table.

Consider choosing a different tablecloth for each month. Make space for a candle, and think about buying some different coloured candles to match the months' moods. Spend some time at the beginning of the month walking or pottering around in the garden and see what you can come up with.

You might consider writing something down at the beginning of each month – an intention, thought or word for the month ahead – and tucking it under a stone or ornament to look at again at the end of the month. And as we are in January, you could do the same for the whole year ahead.

Your table this month might include:
- Pieces of moss
- Twigs of oak and ash, to compare and learn the differences
- Lichen
- Seed heads
- Feathers
- Stones and pebbles
- Candles in white or blue

Light your candle each morning in January, while the mornings are dark. Take a moment to think about this still, quiet moment in the year, to enjoy the dark and the cold, and the cosiness of your candle glowing in the dark.

GARDENS

Gardening by the moon

Just as the moon moves the earth's water to create tides, some believe that it has other effects on the natural world. If it can move oceans, perhaps it can move ground water too, and even the water trapped in the roots and stems of a plant. Planting by the moon is a method of gardening that taps into the moon's phases with this in mind, and allocates tasks according to whether the moon is drawing water and energy upwards – for instance at the full moon when the sun, earth and moon are all in line – or whether the moon's pull is waning.

This almanac makes no claims on the efficacy of planting by the moon, but if you would like to give it a try, the relevant dates and jobs are included for each month. For moon-gardening cynics these sections also work as a guide to the month's gardening if you disregard the exact dates.

Full moon to last quarter: 27th December 2023–3rd January and 26th January–2nd February

A 'drawing down' energy. This phase is a good time for sowing and planting any crops that develop below ground: root crops, bulbs and perennials.

- Chit seed potatoes.
- Plant garlic and rhubarb crowns if the ground is not frozen.
- Sow onions and leeks in seed trays.
- Plant fruit trees and bushes, hedging and bare root rose bushes.

Last quarter to new moon: 4th–11th January (until 11.57)

A dormant period, with low sap and poor growth. Do not sow or plant. A good time though for pruning, while sap is slowed. Weeding now will check growth well. Harvest any crops for storage. Fertilise and mulch the soil. Garden maintenance.

- Prune apple, pear, medlar and quince trees.
- Prune autumn-fruited raspberries, red and white currants, and gooseberries.

- Prune wisteria, cutting back long growths to 2–3 buds and avoiding flower buds.
- Clean and oil tools. Clean pots.
- Check your soil's pH level. If it is low (below 6.5) this would be a good time to add lime or calcified seaweed.
- Weed beds ahead of spring. Mulch areas that have not been recently limed with organic matter.
- Set up your propagator.

New moon to first quarter: 11th (from 11.57)–17th January

The waxing of the moon is associated with rising vitality and upward growth. Towards the end of this phase, plant and sow anything that develops crops above ground. Prepare for growth.

- You could sow chillies and aubergines in a heated propagator. Sow first early peas and sweet peas in pots in the greenhouse, and broad beans outside under cover.
- Buy seeds and prepare seed trays or plugs and compost.
- Place forcers over rhubarb plants to exclude light and draw up stems.

First quarter to full moon: 18th–25th January

This is the best time for sowing crops that develop above ground, but is bad for root crops. Take cuttings and make grafts but avoid all other pruning. Fertilise.

- Sow chillies and aubergines indoors in a heated propagator.
- Sow broad beans straight into the ground if it is not frozen, and cover them with cloches.
- Sow hardy first early peas and sweet peas in pots under cover.

Note: Where no specific time for the change between phases is mentioned, this is because it happens outside of usual gardening hours. For exact changeover times for any late-night or pre-dawn gardening, refer to the January moon phase chart on page 18.

GARDEN CRAFT

Ice sun-catchers

Make use of the low temperatures by making these ice ornaments to catch the winter sun.

You will need:
> Paper plates
> Shot glasses, filled with pebbles
> A jug of water
> Berries, leaves, flowers
> Ribbon

Place your shot glass in the centre of the paper plate. Pour water onto the plate and then arrange the leaves, berries and flowers. Leave outside overnight. In the morning if the water has frozen you can peel off the paper plate and loop the ribbon through the hole left by the shot glass. Hang it in a place where it will catch the sun.

NATURE

Garden wildlife in January

Most garden wildlife is still hibernating, tucked up beneath leaves, in compost heaps or log piles, waiting out winter. But it's not uncommon to spot occasional signs of activity. A hedgehog might rouse itself from hibernation on mild evenings, in search of food, or you could spot a frog at the bottom of the pond. On dry, sunny days, red admiral butterflies can be found basking on a sunny wall, while honeybee hives buzz with the year's tentative first activity. But, for the most part, the garden is quiet, kept alive only by the activities of birds.

It might not look like a significant change, but the gradual lengthening of days after the winter solstice triggers birds into the beginnings of breeding activity. Signs will be subtle at first but you may spot magpies gathering sticks as a sort of trial run for the real deal in a few weeks' time, and tits entering and pecking at the holes of nest boxes. If you have a nest box and you haven't put it up yet, now's the time to do it.

It's amazing that birds have time to think about breeding when there are so few hours to find food. While day length is increasing slowly, small birds like tits and wrens are still spending most hours of daylight looking for food. These small birds have a high body temperature (around 40°C) and it takes a lot of calories to maintain that in cold weather.

Beneath the soil you might think nothing is happening, but plans are being made for summer: if temperatures are above 10°C, then tree roots of young trees will continue to grow, although less vigorously. This is the moment for them to put on growth that will sustain them in future weeks, months and years. They power away, unseen, while the rest of the garden sleeps.

THE KITCHEN

Cooking from the garden in January

Here are some crops that you might find in the kitchen garden
this month: forced rhubarb, purple-sprouting broccoli,
carrots, Brussels sprouts, turnips, beetroot, kale, chard, leeks,
Jerusalem artichokes, lettuces, chicory, radicchio, endive,
cauliflowers, cabbages, celeriac, swedes, winter savory, parsley,
chervil, coriander, rosemary, bay and sage, apples, pears.

Ideas for eating from the garden this month
- Steamed purple-sprouting broccoli sprinkled with
  breadcrumbs that have been fried with garlic and chilli
  until crunchy.
- A 'winter tabbouleh' – shredded kale, carrot, spring onion
  and a big handful of parsley mixed with cooked bulgur
  wheat, lemon juice and olive oil.
- Swede, carrot and potato mash (lots of butter) with a
  slow-cooked lamb casserole.
- Beetroot quartered then roasted and dressed with vinegar,
  with winter salad leaves and grilled smoked mackerel.
- Baked rhubarb with Greek yogurt and crumbled
  ginger snaps.

SNACK OF THE MONTH

Haggis pakoras

Every month in this almanac you will find a 'snack of the month'. Not a wholesome sit-down meal for the family, nor a plate that fulfils your nutritional needs – no. These are the salty, crispy, deep-fried nibbly bits that you shouldn't eat between meals; flavourful morsels that ruin your appetite and go best of all with a glass of something, perhaps in front of the telly.

Haggis pakoras emerged from Scotland's vibrant Indian and Pakistani restaurant scene. The almost inevitable fusion of Scotland's love of spices, haggis and putting things in the deep-fryer. They work just as well with vegetarian haggis. Make them for Burns Night – the celebration of Scottish poet Robert Burns, whose birthday, 25th January, is celebrated with food, drink and poetry readings throughout Scotland – or cook them using your Burns Night leftovers.

Makes 12 pakoras
100g buckwheat flour
100g cornflour
1 tablespoon salt
1 tablespoon cayenne pepper
1 tablespoon ground turmeric
1 tablespoon cumin seeds, toasted
1 tablespoon fennel seeds, toasted
1 teaspoon ground cardamom
450g haggis, traditional or vegetarian, defrosted if frozen
rapeseed oil, for frying

For the dip

4 tablespoons natural yogurt

a handful of fresh mint leaves, finely chopped

1 tablespoon white wine vinegar

1 teaspoon sugar

1 small garlic clove, finely grated

salt and pepper, to taste

Method

Make the batter for the pakoras by combining the buckwheat flour, cornflour, salt and spices in a bowl. Whisk in 350ml water to make a smooth and relatively thick mixture.

Cut the haggis into 12 pieces, about 2cm each.

Combine all the dip ingredients in a bowl and season to taste.

Fill a deep pan or deep-fat fryer one-third full with rapeseed oil and heat it to 180°C, or until a cube of bread dropped into it turns golden brown in 15 seconds.

In batches of 4, dip the haggis pieces into the batter to completely coat them, then carefully add them to the pan and fry for about 2 minutes, or until golden, turning them halfway to colour them evenly. Lift them out and leave to drain on a plate lined with kitchen paper. Repeat with the remaining batches. Serve the pakoras while they are hot, with the dip alongside.

FOLK SONG

'The Painful Plough'
Traditional, arr. Richard Barnard

This year's folk songs all reference the garden and gardeners. Plough Monday, the first Monday after Epiphany, which this year falls on 8th January, was the day farm hands returned to work after the Christmas break, and this song is a discussion between a ploughman and a gardener. After the winter ploughing 'through stormy winds and cold' the gardener argues that the gardening trade is best, while the ploughman argues that ploughing is the more important trade. The tune harks back to a 'North Country Ballad', a folk song collected in the 1890s.

Come all you jolly ploughmen of courage stout and bold
Who labour all the winter through stormy winds and cold,
To clothe the fields with plenty, the farmyards to renew
And crown with glad contentment, behold the painful
    plough.

'Hold, ploughman!' says the gardener, 'count not your
    trade with ours,
Come walk you through the garden amongst the lovely
    flowers.
Behold the curious borders, the pleasant walks to view,
There's none such feats of beauty performed by the
    plough.'

'Hold, gardener,' says the ploughman, 'my calling don't
    despise,
For each man for his living upon his trade relies.
O, Adam in the garden was sent to keep it so,
But soon he lost the garden and went to hold the plough.'

So, Adam was a ploughman when ploughing first begun,
The next that did succeed him was Cain his eldest son.
Some of this generation the calling now pursue,
That bread may not be wanted they labour at the plough.

O, Samson was a strong man and Solomon was wise,
And Alexander conquered; he made the world his prize.
King David was a valiant man and many a thousand slew,
But none of all these heroes could live without the plough.

So come you jolly ploughmen of courage stout and bold
Who labour all the winter through stormy winds and cold,
To clothe the fields with plenty, the farmyards to renew,
For all mankind dependeth upon the painful plough.

February

1 St Brigid's Day (Christian)

1 1st–2nd: Imbolc, celebration of beginning of spring, cross-quarter day (Gaelic/Pagan)

1 Start of LGBT+ History Month

2 Candlemas (Christian)

5 St Brigid's Day bank holiday, Ireland

9 Lunar New Year's Eve

10 Chinese New Year, Year of the Green Wood Dragon begins

12 Shrove Monday/Collop Monday/Peasen Monday/Nickanan Night (Christian/traditional)

13 Shrove Tuesday/pancake day (Christian/traditional)

14 Ash Wednesday – start of Lent (Christian)

14 St Valentine's Day

15 Lord Buddha's Parinirvana Day (Buddhist)

FEBRUARY IN THE GARDEN

The earth is still bare, the morning sun still fringes the blades of grass in a silver rime, but some plants are throwing caution to the wind and hats into rings now – this is their moment. Crocuses the colour of dusk sky and egg yolk open their little cups to daintily hold a measure of cold air. Aconites strew golden constellations across lawns and borders, disdaining boundaries. Primroses and sweet violets are blooming and will be visited this month by the odd bumblebee, out gambolling for pollen, zoning in somehow despite their slaloming flight path, and returning home with sunshine-yellow saddlebags.

Above all, though, this is the month of pure, milky white snowdrops – once known as Mary's tapers, Candlemas bells, February fair maids – which mass together in a snowy shimmer. They have been goaded into flower this early by the promise of a temporal niche. Too dainty to compete with summer flowers and leafy canopies, they have made their peace with the snow and ice, antifreeze coursing through their veins, in order to claim a quota of faint winter sun. They are ice queens at heart, though they drop their heads and nod demurely.

With the lengthening days, an urge comes over the gardener to push a seed with the tip of a finger down into soft compost, to usher in life, to start the year. But too little has changed – there is still long to go. Instead, a stalling activity: seed packets stuffed into padded envelopes drop onto door mats; they are spread out on kitchen tables next to steaming cups of tea in slanting rays of low sun – mangetout and cherry tomatoes, marigolds and sunflowers – sorted and timetabled and…not sown…yet. The table surface becomes the garden plot, each rattling packet making promises that only a few will fully keep.

The gardener pulls on boots and gloves and steps outside to harvest those that fulfilled last year's promise: the last of the root veg so long nestled into the earth that it leaves behind an impression of its shape, and the purple sprouting broccoli spears responding to the lengthening days with a stretch of their own.

Garden and weather folklore

Candlemas on the 2nd of February is an important day for
weather divination, with the general theme of the winter
months being 'don't get carried away if it's sunny now…'

> *'If Candlemas Day be dry and fair*
> *The half of the winter is to come, and more*
> *If Candlemas day be wet and foul*
> *The half of the winter is gone at Yule.'*

The most famous manifestation of this is, of course,
Groundhog Day in the US, during which a groundhog emerges
from his burrow. If he 'sees his shadow' – in other words if it is
sunny – he will retreat and spend a further six weeks
underground, as winter will last that long. If he emerges into a
cloudy day, so that he cannot see his shadow, spring will come
early. This is thought to have come to the US from Germany,
where it was a badger rather than a groundhog that was the
focus of the day.

A whole host of saints have been intent on bringing bad
weather in February, according to weather lore. 'St Dorothy
brings the snow' on her feast day on the 6th. St Matthias,
whose feast day was on the 24th (until it was changed in 1969 to
14th May), 'breaks the ice, and if he finds none he will make it'.

Despite all of this alarm about the February weather, we
have our first piece of saint-related gardening advice this
month: 'Beans must be in the clay by Valentine's Day.' This
would have been the hardy fava or field bean, *Vicia faba* – it is
still very much too early to pop your borlottis out.

THE SEA

Average sea temperature in Celcius

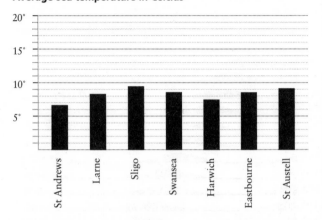

Spring and neap tides

Spring tides are the most extreme tides of the month, with the highest rises and the lowest falls, and they follow a couple of days after the full moon and new moon. These are the times to choose a low tide and go rock-pooling, mudlarking or coastal fossil-hunting. Neap tides are the least extreme, with the smallest movement, and they fall in between the spring tides.

Spring tides: 10th–12th and 25th–27th

Neap tides: 2nd–4th and 17th–19th

Spring tides are shaded in black in the chart opposite.

FEBRUARY

February tide timetable for Dover

For guidance on how to convert this for your local area, see page 8.

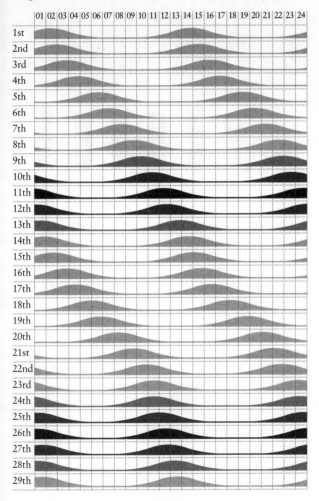

F

37

THE SKY

Stars, meteor showers and planets

Not a great month for bright planet spotting. Venus, Mars and Saturn will become lost in the glare of the sun this month and so will be unobservable. But look out for Jupiter, which will appear high in the southwest sky around 18.00 and will set at about 23.30 in the west.

14th: Close approach of the moon and Jupiter. They will appear in the dusk in the southwest at around 18.00 at about 48 degrees altitude. They will set at 23.30 in the west.

The sun

21st: At solar noon, the sun will reach an altitude of 28 degrees in the London sky and 24 degrees in the Glasgow sky.

Sunrise and set
Coton in the Elms, Derbyshire

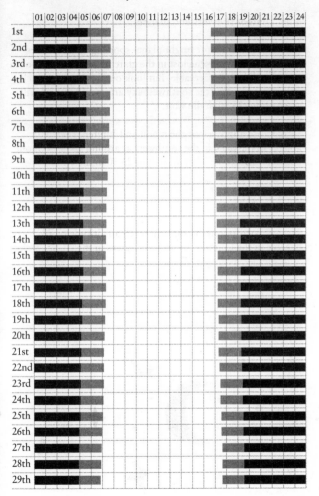

Moonrise and set

Like the sun, the moon rises roughly in the east and sets roughly in the west. It rises about 50 minutes later each day. Use the following guide to work out approximate moonrise times.

Full moon: Rises at around sunset time, but opposite the sun, so in the east as the sun sets in the west.
Last quarter: Rises at around midnight, and is at its highest point as the sun rises.
New moon: Rises at sunrise, in the same part of the sky as the sun, and so cannot be seen.
First quarter: Rises at around noon, and is at its highest point as the sun sets.

Moon phases

Last quarter – 2nd February, 23.18

New moon – 9th February, 22.59

First quarter – 16th February, 15.00

Full moon – 24th February, 12.30

The times given above are for the exact moment each moon phase occurs, for instance the moment that the moon is at its fullest.

February's full moon is known as the Snow Moon, Ice Moon or Storm Moon. As the last full moon before the spring equinox, this moon is also the Lenten Moon.

Moon phases for February

1st	2nd	3rd	4th	5th
6th	7th	8th	9th NEW	10th
11th	12th	13th	14th	15th
16th	17th	18th	19th	20th
21st	22nd	23rd	24th FULL	25th
26th	27th	28th	29th	

MEDITATIONS

February's influences and guidance from Louise Press

February heralds the first signs of spring. The first Celtic fire festival of the year, Imbolc, takes place on the 1st–2nd and celebrates the return of life to the land and to the spirit. What joy an emerging snowdrop can conjure after a long winter. The word Imbolc is believed by some to be from the old Irish 'I mbolg' meaning 'in the belly', referring to the pregnancy of ewes at this time and the stirrings of new life. February is full of promise. The promise of creation and of love is celebrated by many on the 14th, St Valentine's Day.

This month is all about finding the magic in the moment, noticing the extraordinary in the everyday. The days are full of little joys if we take the time to tune into our senses. Look down to notice ice-patterned puddles; listen to the rustle of the little wren darting through the undergrowth; face the sun and feel its warmth on your skin; smell the elusive scent of winter-flowering honeysuckle…these are the gifts of February when life happens in the details.

As we begin to emerge from the dreaming of midwinter, the lunar cycle is here to support our endeavours. The moon begins a new cycle on the 9th in the hopeful and innovative sign of Aquarius. This new moon invites us to review our lives and explore where old patterns hold us back. Where might we be able to shift old habits to make space for the new? Remember, we are still gently waking, peeping one toe out from under the blankets. This is when we experience our wildest dreams. Our ideas feel unbounded and possibility can seem endless.

As is often the way, the full moon on the 24th brings us back to reality with a start. The moon reaches her peak in the sign of Virgo, who is discerning and meticulous. Under this full moon we will be tasked with choosing which dreams to keep in our imagination and which to take action on. A full moon in Virgo helps us to see with clarity.

Making a space for February

There may be little change in the nature table this month, but
try to include some signs of the earth turning, and the new
bulbs starting to shoot. If you are lucky you may have the first
snowdrops out now. It is supposedly unlucky to bring them
indoors on any day except Candlemas, 2nd February, but you
can at least bring in a few then, and you might want to risk
keeping them in for longer. A lovely way to enjoy them is to
dig up a little clump in flower and pot it temporarily into a
terracotta pot, topped with moss, in which case they are still
half outdoors, really.

Your table this month might include:
  • White candles for St Brigid and Candlemas
  • St Brigid's cross made of reeds for St Brigid's day
  • Snowdrops
  • A little vase of winter honeysuckle
  • Lichened bark
  • Feathers
  • Pebbles

It is still dark enough in the mornings to light a candle, but it
won't be so for long. Try to enjoy these dark and cosy
moments in the year before they have passed, rather than
wishing them away too fast. St Brigid is the patron saint of
many things including craft and poetry, so you might include a
little piece of something you have made yourself, such as some
embroidery or crochet, or even a poem.

GARDENS

Gardening by the moon

The following is a guide to gardening with the phases of the moon, according to traditional practices. For moon-gardening cynics it also works as a guide to the month's gardening if you disregard the exact dates.

Full moon to last quarter: 26th January–2nd February and 24th February (from 12.30)–3rd March (until 15.23)

A 'drawing down' energy. This phase is a good time for sowing and planting any crops that develop below ground: root crops, bulbs and perennials.

- Plant Jerusalem artichokes, garlic, rhubarb crowns and shallot and onion sets if the ground is not frozen.
- Sow onions and leeks in seed trays.
- Plant fruit trees and bushes, grapevines, hedging and rose bushes.
- Chit seed potatoes.

Last quarter to new moon: 3rd–9th February

A dormant period, with low sap and poor growth. Do not sow or plant. A good time though for pruning, while sap is slowed. Weeding now will check growth well. Harvest any crops for storage. Fertilise and mulch the soil. Garden maintenance.

- Prune apple, pear, medlar and quince trees.
- Prune autumn-fruited raspberries, red and white currants, and gooseberries.
- Prune wisteria, cutting back long growths to 2–3 buds and avoiding flower buds.
- Clean and oil tools. Clean pots.
- Weed beds ahead of spring. Mulch them with organic matter. Prepare for planting out.

F

New moon to first quarter: 10th–16th February
The waxing of the moon is associated with rising vitality and upward growth. Towards the end of this phase, plant and sow anything that develops crops above ground. Prepare for growth.

- Sow chillies and aubergines, broad beans and first early peas, or wait for the first-quarter phase, which is more suited to sowing.
- Buy seeds and prepare seed trays or plugs and compost.
- Place forcers over rhubarb plants to exclude light and draw up the stems.
- Give spring cabbages and other brassicas a high-nitrogen feed.

First quarter to full moon: 17th–24th February (until 12.30)
This is the best time for sowing crops that develop above ground, but is bad for root crops. Take cuttings and make grafts but avoid all other pruning. Fertilise.

- Sow early lettuces, winter salad leaves, spinach, radishes, hardy first early peas and early varieties of Brussels sprouts, kohlrabi and sprouting broccoli in pots under cover.
- Sow broad beans straight into the ground if it is not frozen, and cover them with cloches.
- Sow chillies and aubergines indoors in a heated propagator.

Note: Where no specific time for the change between phases is mentioned, this is because it happens outside of usual gardening hours. For exact changeover times for any late-night or pre-dawn gardening, refer to the February moon phase chart on page 40.

GARDEN CRAFT

Snölykta (Snow lantern)

Making a *snölykta* is a Swedish tradition during the long
northern winter, creating a welcoming snow lantern for a front
lawn. It is traditionally made in the form of a hollow cone
about a metre in width and height, formed from snowballs, but
you can make smaller glowing snow lanterns any time there is
enough snow on the ground to make the snowballs for it.

You will need:
   Candles (or LED fairy lights)

Start making snowballs and arranging them in a circle on the
ground – make it larger or smaller depending on the amount of
snow you have. Build up the walls using more snowballs,
tapering the snow lantern into a cone shape and leaving good
gaps in between the snowballs where the light can shine
through. Once you have nearly reached the top, lower in one or
more lit candles, depending on how large the base is. You could
use LED fairy lights instead here, switching them on before
you lower them into the cone. Finish off the top with more
snowballs.

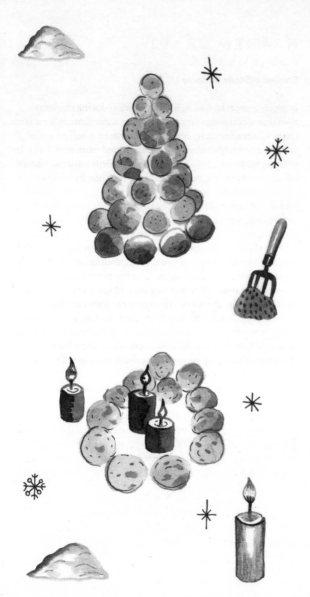

NATURE

Garden wildlife in February

It might not seem like it, but February is the month when hormones in garden birds start to rage, and breeding activity steps up another gear. Males and females are pairing up, courting behaviour begins in earnest and territories are being established and defended. Look out for wood pigeons, which pair for life, preening each other from a tree branch or house roof. Many garden species, including tits, robins and blackbirds, rekindle relationships with previous mates rather than find a new one, but unpaired birds will be on the lookout for someone to procreate with and will be singing for attention in earnest. It's National Nest box Week during 14–21 February, as this is your last chance to get nest boxes up before nesting actually begins.

Below ground there are tentative signs of spring. Some bumblebee queens will be rousing from hibernation this month, feeding from flowers such as crocus and willow, the nectar from which gives them the energy to fly and look for a nest site. Once they have found a suitable spot – often a hole in the ground, clump of tussocky grass, bird box or space beneath a garden shed – they will eat pollen to activate their ovaries, and then use sperm stored from mating the previous summer to fertilise eggs that become their first batch of workers.

This batch of eggs is laid on a mound of wax, secreted from the queen's body and mixed with pollen. She also makes a wax pot and fills it with nectar. Like a bird, she keeps her eggs warm by sitting on them and shivering her muscles, and she drinks nectar from the pot so she doesn't have to leave the nest for food. After a few days, tiny bee larvae hatch from the eggs. The queen starts leaving the nest to collect pollen and nectar to feed to the larvae. After around two weeks, they spin a cocoon and develop into adult bees, by which time the queen is already busy feeding her next batch of grubs.

THE KITCHEN

F

Cooking from the garden in February

Here are some crops that you might find in the kitchen
garden this month: forced rhubarb, purple sprouting
broccoli, carrots, Brussels sprouts, turnips, beetroot, spinach,
Jerusalem artichokes, kale, chard, lettuces, chicory, radicchio,
puntarelle, endive, cauliflowers, cabbages, celeriac, swedes,
leeks, winter savory, parsley, chervil, coriander, rosemary, bay,
sage, apples, pears.

Ideas for eating from the garden this month
- Raw beetroot and carrot grated and marinated together
  in orange juice, vinegar, oil, salt and pepper, before
  mixing in orange segments and topping with toasted
  seeds to serve.
- Savoy cabbage fried in butter with coriander seeds until
  caramelised, and then a bit of cream stirred in, served
  with sausages.
- Cauliflower florets broken up and roasted in olive oil,
  cumin and coriander, with salted and herbed yogurt.
- Buckwheat crêpes with spinach and ricotta filling.
- Carrot cake made with apple purée and lots of
  cardamom, with cardamom cream cheese frosting.

SNACK OF THE MONTH

Wild garlic and nori crackers

These popular Chinese New Year snacks are simple to make and incredibly crunchy. They are traditionally made just with seaweed. But towards the end of the month, the wild garlic will emerge, and it makes a wonderful addition if you have it.

Makes about 18 crackers

70g cornflour

1 teaspoon white wine vinegar

2 sheets filo pastry, defrosted if frozen

5 sheets nori seaweed

a handful of wild garlic leaves (if available, or try mustard greens), washed

rapeseed oil, for frying

salt and pepper, to taste

Method

Whisk the cornflour and vinegar in a bowl with 70ml water to make a thin batter. Using a sharp knife or scissors, cut the filo sheets and nori sheets into similar-sized squares, about 7 × 7cm.

Take a piece of filo, brush it with the batter using a pastry brush, then place a nori sheet on top. Brush with batter again, place a piece of wild garlic on top, brush with batter again, then place another layer of filo on top. Press down the edges to seal them, then brush with batter again. Fold the whole thing in half like a book, then cut it in half horizontally. This will create layers for the hot oil to get between, bubble up and make crispy.

Fill a deep pan or deep-fat fryer one-third full with oil and heat it to 180°C, until a cube of bread dropped in turns golden in 15 seconds. Carefully add the crackers one by one and fry for 10 seconds on each side, until light brown. Lift them out and leave to drain on a plate lined with kitchen paper. Season with salt and pepper and leave to cool a little before serving.

Plum shuttles for Valentine's Day

These traditional Valentine's treats are thought to date back to a time when weaving by hand loom and shuttle was common in many houses. Plum was the traditional word for raisins until the 18th century. Bake them and give one – or more – to your true love.

Makes 12 small buns

½ teaspoon dried yeast
1 teaspoon caster sugar
100ml milk, plus extra to baste
25g unsalted butter
250g bread flour, plus extra for kneading
pinch of salt
zest of 1 orange
60g raisins
1 tablespoon granulated sugar
1 teaspoon caraway seeds, freshly ground

Method

In a small bowl, mix the yeast, sugar and 25ml warm water. Leave to froth for 15 minutes. Warm the milk and butter over a low heat for 2–3 minutes. Add the flour and salt to a large bowl, add the warm milk and yeast and knead together into a smooth dough. Add the zest and raisins and bring together. Turn onto a well-floured surface and knead for another few minutes, using more flour if necessary. Return to the bowl, cover and leave somewhere warm to double in size, for about 2 hours.

Knock the air out of the dough, give another knead, then separate into 12 oval-shaped pieces, thinner at one end. Spread out on lined baking trays, cover with a clean tea towel and leave somewhere warm to rise for 30 minutes. Preheat the oven to 200°C, Gas Mark 6, and brush the buns with milk. Mix together the sugar and caraway seeds and scatter over the buns, then bake for 30 minutes. Allow to cool before eating.

FOLK SONG

'Green Grows the Laurel'
Traditional, arr. Richard Barnard

This song for Valentine's Day is about losing a lover and wanting them back, and it references violets, February's birth flower. The song employs the Victorian idea of the 'language of flowers', with violets representing loyalty and faithfulness. The melody is close to a Romany version collected in Hampshire in the 1900s.

I once had a true love but now I have none and since he has left me I sigh all a-lone; and since he has left me con-tent I must be, for he now loves a-no-ther one bet-ter than me. *So green grows the laur-el and so does the yew and sor-ry I was when I part-ed from you, but on your re-turn-ing our love will be new and I'll change the green lau-rels for vio-lets so blue.*

I once had a true love but now I have none
And since he has left me I sigh all alone;
And since he has left me content I must be,
For he now loves another one better than me.
So green grows the laurel and so does the yew
And sorry I was when I parted from you,
But on your returning our love will be new
And I'll change the green laurels for violets so blue.

I wrote him a letter in red, rosy lines.
He wrote me his answer with words so entwined
Saying, 'Keep your love letter and I will keep mine,
You write to your true love and I'll write to mine.'
So green grows the laurel and so does the yew
And sorry I was when I parted from you,
But on your returning our love will be new
And I'll change the green laurels for violets so blue.

I passed my love's window both early and late
And the looks that he gave me my poor heart would break;
The looks that he gave me ten thousand would kill,
But wherever I go I will be his love still.
So green grows the laurel and so does the yew
And sorry I was when I parted from you,
But on your returning our love will be new
And I'll change the green laurels for violets so blue.

GARDEN SPECIAL

Spring nectar-rich plants

Insects are in decline, and as they are at the bottom of the food chain, their decreasing numbers impact all other forms of wildlife: birds, bats, hedgehogs and all. Happily, gardeners are in a brilliant position to help, by planting pollen-rich flowers in the garden. In this almanac there are four special double-page spreads to help you identify pollen-rich plants for every season, so that the insects in your garden never go without.

In spring, insects are in great need of sustenance, with some such as queen bumblebees having just emerged from overwintering, depleted from the lack of food, and needing energy to feed their new brood. Early sources of pollen can be the difference between life and death of a nest.

This being a good planting time, look ahead to the 'nectar-rich plant' pages for the other seasons (see pages 122, 190 and 258) to get ideas on what to plant now, for future nectar.

Primrose, *Primula vulgaris*: Often among the first flowers in the garden and visited on mild spring days by early bumblebees.
Crocus, *Crocus vernus*: An early-flowering bulb that offers insects lots of nectar. Plant close to the base of early-blossoming fruit trees to help draw insects towards the blossom – they will pollinate your trees and give you a greater harvest, while taking nourishment for themselves.
Grape hyacinth, *Muscari armeniacum*: Little bright blue spikes of cup-like flowers, each containing nectar. Very well visited by early emerging insects.
Dead-nettle, *Lamium*: A perennial with nettle-like foliage but no sting, hence the common name. Small but pollen-rich flowers.
Lungwort, *Pulmonaria*: Perennials for the border, they produce pretty and pollen-heavy blue and pink flowers that emerge early in the year.

LUNGWORT

DEAD-
NETTLE

PRIMROSE

GRAPE HYACINTH

CROCUS

March

1 St David's Day – patron saint of Wales

5 St Piran's Day – patron saint of Cornwall

8 International Women's Day

8 St John of God's Day – patron saint of booksellers

10 Mothering Sunday/fourth Sunday in Lent (traditional/Christian)

10 Ramadan (Islamic month of fasting, prayer and reflection) – begins at sundown

17 17th–18th St Patrick's Day and St Patrick's Day bank holiday, Northern Ireland

20 Spring/vernal equinox, at 03.06 – start of astronomical spring

20 Ostara – Pagan celebration of spring

23 Purim (Jewish holiday) begins at sundown

25 Holi (Hindu spring festival) begins at sundown

31 Easter Sunday (Christian)

31 British Summer Time (BST) and Irish Standard Time (IST) begin – both are Greenwich Mean Time/Coordinated Universal Time + one hour. Clocks go forward one hour at 01.00.

MARCH IN THE GARDEN

Something in the air sets the gardener's senses tingling. The scent of sap bubbling up, daffodils the colour of sunshine, the crisp air. Persephone is wavering, balanced tiptoe on the equinoctial threshold, stepping into spring uncertainly: for every step forward, two steps back. Trees and bushes choose to believe and make themselves vulnerable, tentatively showing sweet green tips and the softest blossom buds from behind their winter armour. March responds carelessly, brutishly, showering them one day in snow, the next in rain, then in warm, glowing, impossibly gorgeous sunshine, then in snow again.

Where last month everything was too early, suddenly it is nearly too late. Every seed must be sown. The gardener, seized by purpose, grabs dibbers, labels and rattling handfuls of seeds. The packets are ripped open, each seed containing the entire plant in miniature – food and mineral reserves, enzymes and hormones, everything needed to create a full-grown plant, bar the coming summer's many hours of sunlight and rainfall. The seed is pushed into the compost and padded carefully over, then water is trickled in after it so that the dampened compost clings to it. The seed swells and begins its journey towards leaves and petals and fruit.

That's the easy part, because now begins the annual obstacle course. Will the seeds fall to the gnawing snail, be bundled away by the hungry mouse? Will the air around the seedlings be too still and allow grey mould to linger and thicken? Will the light be too low, or too harsh? Will the gardener, so keen now, so full of good intentions, forget to tie them up when they start to flop, or to feed them? Will the neighbour entrusted with watering them over a hot weekend simply wave the watering can absent-mindedly towards them, leaving roots pulling in vain and leaves crinkling?

No, says March, winking its green eye – this time it will be different. The gardener, who is a fool for this moment, falls for it again in the equinox sun, as they step optimistically into the light half of the year.

Garden and weather folklore

Some very specific sowing directions come from the saints this month, as you might expect for a month so crucial to agriculture.

'On St David's Day [1st], put oats and barley in the clay' – perhaps not a crop many of us are sowing, but this is a sign that the soil is starting to warm up, at least for the hardier crops. Two more saints quickly follow, with more useful advice. St Gregory's original feast day of 12th March (which was changed in the 1960s to 3rd September) is the day when we are supposed to sow our onions; Gregory the Great is so associated with onions that he was known in Lancashire as Gregory-gret-Onion. And St Benedict's Day, celebrated by monks on 21st March (though by the Catholic Church on 11th July), is the day to get your maincrop peas into the ground.

Good Friday, which falls on 29th March this year, is the traditional day to plant potatoes and parsley. When potatoes were brought to Europe from Peru in the 16th century, many Protestants refused to plant them because they were not mentioned in the Bible. Irish Catholics decided that planting them was acceptable as long as it was done on Good Friday and they were sprinkled with holy water. Good Friday is also always a root day when gardening by the moon (though with such an early Easter, this timing might not be so sensible in 2024). Parsley was thought to take so long to germinate because its root had to travel to hell and back seven times before it would sprout. Planting the parsley on Good Friday – when the Devil has no jurisdiction over the soil – was the key.

We don't want warm weather too soon, according to weather lore: 'When the apple blooms in March, for the fruit you'll search.' Watch out for a spell of cold weather at the end of the month which coincides with the blackthorn blossom and is known as a 'blackthorn winter'. Also be wary on 29th, 30th and 31st March, as these are the 'borrowed days', believed in Irish custom to have been borrowed from April. They are said to bring about a wintry relapse. Snowfall this month is called a 'lambing storm', and is expected – or perhaps hoped – to be brief.

THE SEA

Average sea temperature in Celcius

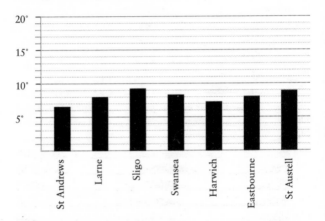

Spring and neap tides

Spring tides are the most extreme tides of the month, with the highest rises and the lowest falls, and they follow a couple of days after the full moon and new moon. These are the times to choose a low tide and go rock-pooling, mudlarking or coastal fossil-hunting. Neap tides are the least extreme, with the smallest movement, and they fall in between the spring tides.

Spring tides: 11th–13th and 26th–28th

Neap tides: 4th–6th and 18th–20th

Spring tides are shaded in black in the chart opposite.

March tide timetable for Dover

For guidance on how to convert this for your local area, see page 8.

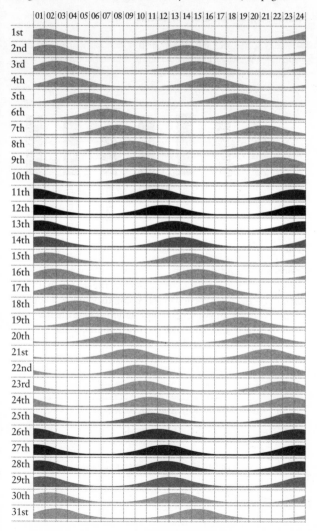

M

THE SKY

Stars, meteor showers and planets

Mercury is not an easy planet to spot as it lies so close to the sun that it gets lost in the sun's glare, but it will be at its furthest from the sun this month. Venus, Mars and Saturn will remain unobservable, lying too close to the direction of the sun. Throughout the month Jupiter will get steadily closer to the glare of the sun, too.

13th: Close approach of the moon and Jupiter. They will appear in the dusk in the southwest at around 18.30. They will set at 22.20 in the northwest.
24th: Mercury's greatest elongation east, when it is furthest from the sun and easiest to see. Visible for a few days either side of this date. In the evening, look in the direction of sunset close to the horizon from about 19.00, as the dusk fades.

The sun

17th: Equilux. It is commonly believed that day and night are of equal length on the equinox. This is not quite the case, because we measure day length using the moment the top of the sun appears over or disappears below the horizon, rather than the moment the centre of the sun is on the horizon. Equilux is when day and night are actually the same length. It occurs around 17th March this year in the UK and Ireland.
20th: Spring equinox. The vernal or spring equinox falls at 03.06. This is the moment at which the centre of the sun is directly above the equator. It will occur again at the autumn equinox in September.
20th: At solar noon the sun will reach an altitude of 38 degrees in the London sky and 34 degrees in the Glasgow sky.

Sunrise and set

Coton in the Elms, Derbyshire

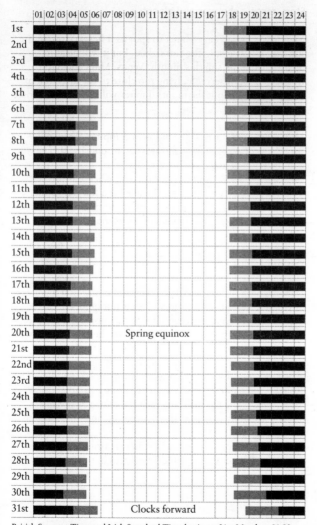

Spring equinox

Clocks forward

British Summer Time and Irish Standard Time begin on 31st March at 01.00 and this has been accounted for above

Moonrise and set

Like the sun, the moon rises roughly in the east and sets roughly in the west. It rises about 50 minutes later each day. Use the following guide to work out approximate moonrise times.

Full moon: Rises at around sunset time, but opposite the sun, so in the east as the sun sets in the west.
Last quarter: Rises at around midnight, and is at its highest point as the sun rises.
New moon: Rises at sunrise, in the same part of the sky as the sun, and so cannot be seen.
First quarter: Rises at around noon, and is at its highest point as the sun sets.

Moon phases

Last quarter – 3rd March, 15.23	
New moon – 10th March, 09.00	
First quarter – 17th March, 04.11	
Full moon – 25th March, 07.00	

The times given above are for the exact moment each moon phase occurs.

March's full moon is known as the Plough Moon, the first full moon following the 'ecclesiastical spring equinox'. It is also the Paschal Moon, that dictates the timing of Easter Sunday.

On 25th March this year there will be a penumbral lunar eclipse of the full moon, which is when the moon moves through the faint, outer part of the earth's shadow. It will be visible from the Americas and Asia, but not the UK and Ireland where it will occur beneath the horizon.

Moon phases for March

1st	2nd	3rd	4th	5th
6th	7th	8th	9th	10th NEW
11th	12th	13th	14th	15th
16th	17th	18th	19th	20th
21st	22nd	23rd	24th	25th FULL
26th	27th	28th	29th	30th
31st				

MEDITATIONS

March's influences and guidance from Louise Press

March…the great awakening! It is time to uncurl from our winter sleep and turn to face the warming sun. Now we begin to manifest the ideas and creations that have been born out of our dreaming of recent weeks. Let's learn from the wisdom of nature's cycles and be guided by all we witness around us. Take note of the courageous daffodils that emerge no matter what the weather throws at them. Now is the time to push our own heads up and out of the soil in the knowledge that we are deeply rooted. It's time to dare to share our calling with the world, to take risks and journey forth.

The 10th March welcomes the new moon in Pisces, offering us a wonderful opportunity to take a final deep dive into the dream world, to retrieve any pearls of wisdom waiting to be strung into a necklace of opportunity for the year ahead. Pisces is a sensitive sign, reminding us to take care of ourselves as we follow our intuition into the expansion of spring.

The spring equinox falls on 20th March, the festival of Ostara. We find ourselves in a perfect moment of balance – equi (equal) plus nox (night) equals light and dark, masculine and feminine, conscious and unconscious, rest and action. This balance and subsequent tipping point come at the moment in the year when we transition from our inner world of dreaming to the outer world of action. We are supported in these endeavours with more daylight for the task in hand.

Following the equinox, our moon will be full in the shadow of the penumbral eclipse on the 25th. Beautifully aligned with the theme of balance and equality, the full moon is in the sign of Libra, the scales. This harmonious energy can encourage us to spring clean; to clear the clutter and to cleanse ourselves in preparation for the lighter, longer days ahead. Clarity of thought and action is supported by a clear environment.

M

Making a space for March

Winter can keep March strongly in its grip, so at the beginning of the month you may struggle to find anything very different from February for your nature table. We all get excited about the lighter days and the growth it will bring, but we need to recognise that March has one foot in winter and one in spring. Arrange your table to reflect that, and include some of the items from your winter table, too. But it is time to look out in particular for daffodils starting to bloom, as well as cherry, plum and blackthorn blossom – hopeful signs of brighter days to come.

Your table this month might include:
- Green or pink candles
- A bunch of daffodils
- Branches of blackthorn blossom in a tall vase (cut them before they are in flower and watch them unfurl in the warmth of the house)
- A pot of miniature irises
- Pebbles, twigs, moss and feathers

Try to light your candles each day, but take a moment at the spring equinox, which falls this month on the 20th, to think about how much the items on your table will have changed by the autumn equinox in September. There will be many long, light days to come between now and then.

GARDENS

Gardening by the moon

The following is a guide to gardening with the phases of the moon, according to traditional practices. For moon-gardening cynics it also works as a guide to the month's gardening if you disregard the exact dates.

Full moon to last quarter: 24th February (from 12.30)–3rd March (until 15.23) and 25th March–1st April
A 'drawing down' energy. This phase is a good time for sowing and planting any crops that develop below ground: root crops, bulbs and perennials.

- Plant onion sets, rhubarb crowns, asparagus crowns and Jerusalem artichokes.
- Plant new cold-stored strawberry runners (in milder parts of the country) and sow seeds of alpine strawberries.
- Lift, divide and replant perennial herbs.
- Chit seed potatoes.
- Start planting out first early potatoes.
- In mild areas, sow carrots, turnips, beetroot and radishes, and cover with cloches.
- Lift, split and replant crowded clumps of snowdrops.
- Plant lily and gladioli bulbs and dahlia tubers in pots indoors.

Last quarter to new moon: 3rd (from 15.23)–9th March
A dormant period, with low sap and poor growth. Do not sow or plant. A good time though for pruning, while sap is slowed. Weeding now will check growth well. Harvest any crops for storage. Fertilise and mulch the soil. Garden maintenance.

- Prune raspberries, red and white currants and gooseberries.
- Protect cherry, apricot, peach and nectarine blossom from frosts. Plastic/glass coverings will protect peaches and nectarines from peach leaf curl.
- Feed perennials and overwintering plants – such as onions, kale, cabbages, hardy lettuces and leaves – with liquid feed.

M

- Weed and mulch beds and prepare them for planting out.
- Feed and mulch fruit trees and bushes.
- Make a bean trench: dig out a trench, line it with newspaper and fill with compost and organic waste matter.

New moon to first quarter: 10th–16th March

The waxing of the moon is associated with rising vitality and upward growth. Towards the end of this phase, plant and sow anything that develops crops above ground. Prepare for growth.

- Sow aubergines, tomatoes, chillies and peppers, tomatoes indoors in a heated propagator, along with any of the seeds in the first quarter to full moon phase, or wait for that phase, which is even more suited to sowing.

First quarter to full moon: 17th–24th March

This is the best time for sowing crops that develop above ground, but is bad for root crops. Pot up or plant out seedlings and young plants. Take cuttings and make grafts but avoid all other pruning. Fertilise.

- Sow aubergines, chillies and peppers, cucumbers and tomatoes indoors in a heated propagator.
- Sow Brussels sprouts, summer and autumn cabbages, celery, Florence fennel, lettuces and sprouting broccoli in pots or modules in a cold greenhouse or cold frame.
- Sow hardy annual flower seeds in pots under cover.
- In mild areas and on light soils, direct sow lettuce, maincrop peas, spinach and Swiss chard, and cover with cloches.
- Plant out broad beans and maincrop peas, under cloches.
- Gradually increase feeding and watering of house plants.

Note: Where no specific time for the change between phases is mentioned, this is because it happens outside of usual gardening hours. For exact changeover times for any late-night or pre-dawn gardening, refer to the March moon phase chart on page 64.

GARDEN CRAFT

Ostereierbaum, or Easter egg tree

In Germany and Austria at Eastertide, blossom trees are decorated with hundreds of small Easter egg decorations, hung from ribbons. Some people choose to decorate trees outdoors while others bring a branch indoors. The warmth indoors will encourage the buds to begin to grow and the blossom to bloom.

You will need:
- A branch – cherry, magnolia or blackthorn blossom, corkscrew hazel or pussy willow work particularly well
- A large narrow-necked vase filled with water
- Hanging Easter egg decorations, small pompoms in pastel colours trimmed into egg shapes and/or fluffy chicks
- Pastel-coloured 3mm-wide ribbon
- Pebbles
- Large-eyed needle

Place your branch in the vase (placing pebbles in the bottom of the vase to hold the branch upright if necessary). Use a large-eyed needle to thread lengths of ribbon through the eggs, pompoms and/or chicks, then hang the decorations from the branches using the ribbons.

M

NATURE

Garden wildlife in March

Things are suddenly very busy in our gardens. Bird nesting gathers apace, although this depends on temperature, food and the condition of the birds themselves. Winter is a difficult time for them, and some will be in better shape than others. Those nesting now tend to be older and more experienced, while the younger birds will need another few weeks before they're in prime breeding condition.

Ponds bubble with mating amphibians. Frogs in the southwest start spawning first, with those further north and east joining the party as temperatures increase. Fertilisation is external, with the male frog clasping onto the back of the female in a position called amplexus. Spawn is laid in clumps and eaten by many species, including dragonfly larvae, newts and birds. If you think you have too much frogspawn in your pond, you haven't – most of it will be eaten by predators.

Meanwhile hedgehogs are coming out of hibernation and are hungry. They're known for eating slugs and snails but they're much more likely to feast on caterpillars, beetles and earthworms. Wilder gardens, with plenty of leaf litter, a compost heap, areas of long grass and a log pile, will have the greatest number of invertebrates for hedgehogs to eat.

If you live near the coast, keep an eye out for migrating birds, which can be found refuelling in gardens, as a pit stop on their way to, or from, their destination. At this time of year, redwings and fieldfares are starting to leave the UK for Scandinavia and Russia. Listen out for the 'tseep' of redwings flying overhead, and the 'football rattle' sound of fieldfares. They may spend a few days in gardens, feeding, before their long journey back to their mating grounds, and will benefit from any berries or windfall fruit you have left.

Meanwhile chiffchaffs are arriving, again spending a few days in coastal gardens before heading inland. Notice them teasing the first of the year's aphids off your roses, and their early calls of 'chiff chaff' within a growing dawn chorus.

THE KITCHEN

Cooking from the garden in March

Here are some crops that you might find in the kitchen garden this month: forced rhubarb, purple sprouting broccoli, Brussels sprouts, chicory, kale, onions, radishes, cabbages, cauliflowers, chard, endive, radicchio, lettuces, leeks, spinach, turnips, sorrel, winter savory, parsley, chervil, coriander, rosemary, bay, sage.

Ideas for eating from the garden this month

- Leeks cooked in butter until soft and then with a spoonful of mustard mixed in, along with salt and pepper and a handful of grated cheese, piled onto a piece of toast and grilled.
- Root veg – turnips, beetroot, swede, carrot – cut into chunks and roasted with honey and paprika, then topped with dollops of chipotle mayonnaise and crispy fried onions.
- Soda bread made with chopped wild garlic, then sliced, toasted and buttered.
- Potato and rosemary rösti, topped with a fried egg and served with wilted, buttered spring greens.
- *Kuku sabzi* – Persian herb omelette so thick with finely chopped herbs that it is entirely green, served with salted labneh or thick Greek yogurt, toasted pitta and olives.

SNACK OF THE MONTH

Ajil (Persian trail mix)

Nowruz is the Iranian (or Persian) New Year and is celebrated on the spring equinox, which this year falls on 20th March. The last Wednesday of the old year is called Chaharshanbe Suri ('Scarlet Wednesday') and is a day of great celebration, with bonfires in the streets that people jump over for luck in the coming year, and the banging of pots and pans. *Ajil*, a mixture of dried fruit, nuts and seeds, is the traditional food of the night that everyone nibbles on. This version is sweet and salty – every mouthful is different – as well as moreish and satisfying. It is a very flexible recipe, so vary the ingredients to suit you.

Makes a 1-litre jar

240g good-quality tinned chickpeas, drained

2 tablespoons sesame seeds

2 tablespoons olive oil

100g flaked almonds

100g whole almonds

100g shelled pistachios

100g pumpkin seeds

100g dried cherries

100g dried figs, diced

100g dried mulberries

100g sultanas

salt and pepper, to taste

Method
Preheat the oven to 220°C, Gas Mark 7. Dry the chickpeas thoroughly with kitchen paper or a clean tea towel. When completely dry, add them to a bowl with the sesame seeds and

drizzle with the olive oil and a good pinch of salt and pepper. Mix well with a spoon until everything is evenly coated in oil, then spread the mixture out on a baking tray. Roast for 30 minutes or until crisp and golden, giving the tray a little shake halfway through to help them crisp evenly. Remove and leave to cool.

Meanwhile, heat a dry frying pan. Add the flaked and whole almonds, pistachios and pumpkin seeds to the pan and cook, stirring, until they start to pop and release their nutty aroma. Tip them out into a bowl, then sprinkle with salt and stir.

Allow everything to cool to room temperature, then mix all the ingredients, including the dried cherries, figs, mulberries and sultanas, in a large bowl. You may want to add a little more salt and pepper if you have a savoury tooth, as this goes well with the sweetness of the dried fruit. Serve once cooled, or this can be stored in an airtight container for a couple of weeks.

THE ALMANAC 2024

FOLK SONG

'Down by the Salley Gardens'
Traditional, arr. Richard Barnard

This is a song of remembrance of a youthful time spent with a lover, and of regret for acting in an impetuous manner, and therefore, it appears, losing her. There are references to snow and to growing grass in this song, both of which we might see in the garden in this unpredictable month, though here the snow imagery is used to underline the lover's innocent qualities: 'her little snow-white feet' and her 'snow-white hand'.

The words were written by W B Yeats as an attempt to reconstruct a snippet of song sung to him by an old peasant woman in the village of Ballisodare, Co. Sligo. He wrote it as a poem and it remained that way until 1909 when Herbert Hughes set it to music using the old Irish melody 'The Maids of Mourne Shore'.

76

M

Down by the Salley Gardens
My love and I did meet;
She passed the Salley Gardens
With little snow-white feet.
She bid me take love easy
As the leaves grow on the tree;
But I, being young and foolish,
With her would not agree.

In a field by the river
My love and I did stand
And on my leaning shoulder
She laid her snow-white hand.
She bid me take life easy
As the grass grows on the weirs;
But I was young and foolish
And now am full of tears.

April

1 Easter Monday (Christian) – bank holiday in England, Wales, Northern Ireland, Ireland

1 April Fools' Day

9 Eid al-Fitr (Islamic celebration of the end of Ramadan) begins at sighting of crescent moon

14 St Tiburtius' Day – when cuckoos traditionally start singing (stopping on St John's Day, 24th June)

22 Passover/Pesach (Jewish) begins at sundown, with the Seder feast

23 St George's Day – patron saint of England

23 Start of British asparagus season (ends at summer solstice, 20th June)

APRIL IN THE GARDEN

White clouds scud across the blue sky, and the wind has a new ease about it. The gardener's shoulders unclench, a little. In the garden there is a frivolous softening after the hard, serious stuff of winter. All of the sharp, dark edges now blurred with downy pastel blossom, a fuzz of lime-green shoots, the shooting stars of forsythia. Having masqueraded as almost ordinary garden trees all winter long, magnolias suddenly out themselves as vast painterly splodges of pink and white, and cherries as clouds of future confetti. All that's missing is a gambolling lamb in a pale green ribbon, and perhaps a small scattering of fluffy ducklings.

All of that prettiness has a purpose, and the gardener, standing by the fruit tree, can hear that it has hit its mark. Cherry, apple, pear and plum hum with happy activity, the bees taking all they can carry. In return, they are giving the tree what it needs: a speck of pollen, almost incidental. Just a smudge from another tree is enough to kick-start the process that will end with the gardener up a ladder, head in the leaves, nose filled with scent, fingers cupping, wrist twisting.

The gardener does take a small but exquisite harvest this month: the perennials, which are ready so early only because they have long-nurtured roots, deep and established in the soil. They are plucked just as they respond to spring and start to grow, a trio of delicacies. Sharp, lemony sorrel, sweet and nutty baby artichokes, and the most loved and eagerly awaited of all, asparagus. The first cut is taken on the 23rd – St George's Day, Shakespeare's birthday – and the last on Midsummer's Day. A charmed spell of time in which to be at your peak. The gardener takes just a few, drops them into the steamer (briefly), watches the butter glaze a spear tip, lifts this small green spring harvest, and bites.

Garden and weather folklore

'If it thunders on All Fools' Day, it brings good crops of corn and hay.' This particular old saying about the weather on April Fools' Day might have a little science behind it. Thunderstorms only occur when warm air rises from heated ground, forming highly charged cumulonimbus clouds that produce thunder and lightning. Ground that is warm enough for thunderstorms at this moment in the year suggests an early spring, and the start of a good growing season.

Sayings about St George's Day on the 23rd claim that this is the day green growth begins. An old Estonian adage says, 'With his key George makes the grass grow.' In Lithuanian tradition, George is the keeper of the keys to summer and is asked to make the grass grow and to disperse the clouds.

Something to look out for this month is the budding of the trees. The old saying, 'Oak before ash, in for a splash; ash before oak, in for a soak' suggests that the weather for the coming summer will be drier if oak comes into leaf first.

THE SEA

Average sea temperature in Celcius

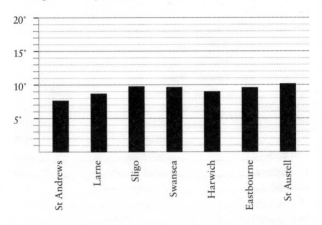

Spring and neap tides

Spring tides are the most extreme tides of the month, with the highest rises and the lowest falls, and they follow a couple of days after the full moon and new moon. These are the times to choose a low tide and go rock-pooling, mudlarking or coastal fossil-hunting. Neap tides are the least extreme, with the smallest movement, and they fall in between the spring tides.

Spring tides: 9th–11th and 24th–26th

Neap tides: 2nd–4th and 16th–18th

Spring tides are shaded in black in the chart opposite.

April tide timetable for Dover

For guidance on how to convert this for your local area, see page 8.

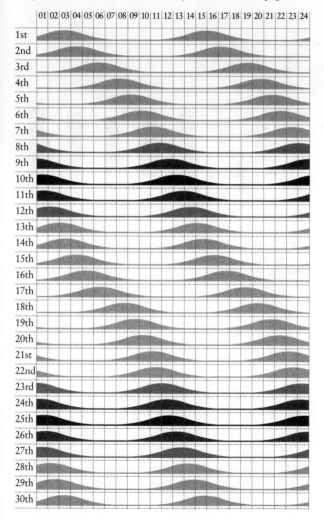

A

THE SKY

Stars, meteor showers and planets

By the end of the month Venus, Mars, Jupiter and Saturn will all lie close to the direction of the sun and will be unobservable.

10th: Brief close approach of the moon and Jupiter. They will appear in the dusk in the west at around 20.30. They will set at 22.00 in the northwest.

The sun

8th: Total eclipse of the sun. It will be visible from northern Mexico, the United States and eastern parts of Canada but not from the UK and Ireland. The partial phase will be visible from the eastern Pacific Ocean, North and Central America excluding Alaska, most of the Caribbean, Greenland and the North Atlantic Ocean.

20th: At solar noon (approximately 13.00 BST/IST) the sun will reach an altitude of 38 degrees in the London sky and 34 degrees in the Glasgow sky.

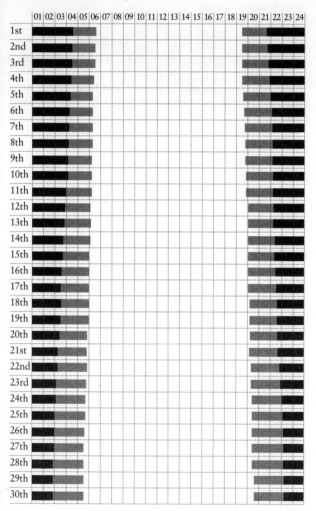

Sunrise and set

Coton in the Elms, Derbyshire

	01 02 03 04 05 06 07 08 09 10 11 12 13 14 15 16 17 18 19 20 21 22 23 24
1st	
2nd	
3rd	
4th	
5th	
6th	
7th	
8th	
9th	
10th	
11th	
12th	
13th	
14th	
15th	
16th	
17th	
18th	
19th	
20th	
21st	
22nd	
23rd	
24th	
25th	
26th	
27th	
28th	
29th	
30th	

A

Moonrise and set

Like the sun, the moon rises roughly in the east and sets roughly in the west. It rises about 50 minutes later each day. Use the following guide to work out approximate moonrise times.

Full moon: Rises at around sunset time, but opposite the sun, so in the east as the sun sets in the west.
Last quarter: Rises at around midnight, and is at its highest point as the sun rises.
New moon: Rises at sunrise, in the same part of the sky as the sun, and so cannot be seen.
First quarter: Rises at around noon, and is at its highest point as the sun sets.

Moon phases

Last quarter – 2nd April, 04.14

New moon – 8th April, 19.20

First quarter – 15th April, 20.13

Full moon – 24th April, 00.48

The times given above are for the exact moment each moon phase occurs, for instance the moment that the moon is at its fullest.

April's full moon is known as the Budding Moon, New Shoots Moon or Seed Moon.

Moon phases for April

1st	2nd	3rd	4th	5th
6th	7th	8th NEW	9th	10th
11th	12th	13th	14th	15th
16th	17th	18th	19th	20th
21st	22nd	23rd	24th FULL	25th
26th	27th	28th	29th	30th

MEDITATIONS

April's influences and guidance from Louise Press

April has the energy of an adolescent…one minute brilliant and promising, the next unpredictable and cantankerous. We are full of creative energy yet there's something about April that can stop us in our tracks. The spring sunshine lifts our hearts and calls forth action, while the April showers and bitter winds can hold us back. It's no coincidence that the month begins with a Fools' Day: April can sometimes take us for fools.

But we can feel the vibrancy of this time rising within us and we are ready to emerge. Surrounded by symbols of new life – the eggs, the lambs and the spring hares – we are encouraged and heartened by the season.

The new moon on 8th April is accompanied by a total solar eclipse, during which the sun, moon and earth will align, making this a powerful time for healing and coming together as one. New moons are a time for setting intentions for the lunar month ahead. We can be guided by astrological signs and seasons, but wishes made during an eclipse are magnified and enriched.

April's new moon in Aries marks the beginning of a new lunar year. Aries, the first sign of the Zodiac, is ruled by Mars, so there may be tantrums. This lunar cycle kicks off with a bang. We can use these young and determined energies to release any blocks that we're putting in our own way.

The full moon on 24th April invites the opportunity for personal growth in the sign of Scorpio. It offers deep transformation by asking us to be curious about what rises from our subconscious to be processed. What constantly niggles us? What negative patterns return again and again? We are being reborn at this time and it's important to be discerning about what we bring with us this time around. There is a strong theme of emergence this month. The seasonal energies and lunar guidance are aligned. What is new for you at this time?

Making a space for April

By now spring is in full swing, and you should be able to pick and choose from a good number of spring blooms for your nature table, and really lean into the pretty pastels of this moment in the year.

A

Your table this month might include:
- Yellow candles
- A pastel-coloured tablecloth
- A little nest filled with colourful eggs
- A vase of cherry blossom
- Miniature spring bulbs, dug up from the garden and potted into little terracotta pots, then topped with moss
- A bunch of small spring flowers in a vase: primroses, muscari, fritillaria
- Pastel-coloured ribbons
- Seeds to be sown this month

Write a word or intention for the month ahead and tuck it somewhere on your table, beneath a stone or a pot. Light the yellow candles and think about the warming sun, and how it has brought all of these flowers into bloom. Consider the seeds you will sow and what they will become.

GARDENS

Gardening by the moon

The following is a guide to gardening with the phases of the moon, according to traditional practices. For moon-gardening cynics it also works as a guide to the month's gardening if you disregard the exact dates.

Full moon to last quarter: 25th March–1st April and 24th April–1st May (until 12.27)
A 'drawing down' energy. This phase is a good time for sowing and planting any crops that develop below ground: root crops, bulbs and perennials.

- Plant second early and maincrop potatoes.
- Sow direct in light soils in warm areas, covering with cloches afterwards: carrots, beetroot, parsnips, turnips, leeks, spring onions.
- Plant out asparagus crowns and globe artichokes, grapevines and strawberries.
- Plant summer-flowering bulbs and tubers: lilies and gladioli.

Last quarter to new moon: 2nd–8th April
A dormant period, with low sap and poor growth. Do not sow or plant. A good time though for pruning, while sap is slowed. Weeding now will check growth well. Harvest any crops for storage. Fertilise and mulch the soil. Garden maintenance.

- Earth up first early potatoes.
- Harvest asparagus, lettuce, rocket and winter salad leaves, spring onions, rhubarb and the last of the purple sprouting broccoli, leeks and kale.
- Start to harden off plants that have been grown indoors, moving them outside during the day and back in at night.
- Create supports for peas by pushing shrubby pea sticks into the ground in a row. Make runner and French bean supports with bamboo canes.
- This is the best time of the month for weeding.
- Cut the lawn.

New moon to first quarter: 9th–15th April

The waxing of the moon is associated with rising vitality and upward growth. Towards the end of this phase, plant and sow anything that develops crops above ground. Prepare for growth.

- Sow any of the seeds in the first quarter–full moon phase towards the end of this period.
- Pot house plants on into the next plant pot size. Water regularly and start feeding fortnightly with liquid feed.
- Prepare ground, mulch and feed soil. Make seed drills and generally prepare.
- Remove covers from forced rhubarb.
- Feed perennials with liquid feed.
- Feed and mulch roses.

First quarter to full moon: 16th–23rd April

This is the best time for sowing crops that develop above ground, but is bad for root crops. Pot up or plant out seedlings and young plants. Take cuttings and make grafts but avoid all other pruning. Fertilise.

- Last chance to sow aubergines, chillies, peppers, melons and tomatoes indoors in a heated propagator.
- In pots under cover for planting out later, sow French beans, runner beans, cabbages, cauliflowers, courgettes, cucumbers, Florence fennel, kale, pumpkins and winter squashes, sweetcorn.
- Sow small amounts of herb seed in pots or seed trays indoors, or direct into the soil under cloches: coriander, chervil, dill and parsley. Sow basil in pots indoors.
- Sow lettuces, maincrop peas, broad beans, rocket, summer purslane, lamb's lettuce, spinach and Swiss chard direct.
- Sow hardy flower seeds outside, in pots or direct.
- Plant up pots and hanging baskets with bedding plants if you can keep them under cover until the danger of frost has passed.

Note: Where no specific time for the change between phases is mentioned, this is because it happens outside of usual gardening hours. For exact changeover times for any late-night or pre-dawn gardening, refer to the April moon phase chart on page 86.

GARDEN CRAFT

A fairy door for May Day Eve

The night of 30th April is May Day Eve, traditionally the time that fairies were out and about (in fact, some attribute Shakespeare's *A Midsummer Night's Dream* as being set on this night, not at midsummer). Fairies were once considered malicious creatures, and it was thought sensible to scatter primrose flowers – which fairies cannot cross – along your home's threshold to prevent them from coming indoors and causing mischief. Perhaps even better to make them a fairy door for a tree, where they can make a home for themselves.

You will need:
    10 flat wooden lollipop sticks
    PVA glue
    Paint
    Acorn cups, tiny pebbles, beads or buttons for the handle
    Pebbles, moss and flowers

Lay eight of the lollipop sticks alongside each other to form the main part of the door. Paint glue all along one side of each of the two leftover sticks and stick them on horizontally to hold the sticks together and to look quirky and fairy-like. Paint the door and stick on an acorn cup, pebble, bead or button as a handle. Nestle it into a nook in the base of a tree, or stick it to the bottom of a fence. Make a little path leading away from the door, and place flowers, pebbles and moss alongside the path to create a fairy garden.

A

NATURE

Garden wildlife in April

This is a month of frenzied bee activity. The solitary red mason bee nests in existing cavities such as the hollow stems of the previous year's plants, airbricks or holes in dead wood made by beetles. Along each nest row, the female makes a series of chambers, using mud. She provisions each chamber with a 'cake' of pollen and nectar, and lays an egg on it, before sealing the cell with more mud. After laying up to 40 eggs, she dies, having never met her offspring. In gardens, red mason bees readily use bee 'hotels', which mimic the natural cavities found in plant stems and dead wood.

Many garden birds are nesting now. Each lays one egg a day, typically at dawn, while the male sings nearby to defend the territory. It's a very noisy month, with blackbirds, song thrushes, tits, robins and wrens all joining together at dawn for a fantastic chorus. The cacophony will peak next month.

Still nest-building will be the long-tailed tits, for whom the process takes a whopping three weeks. Long-tailed tits' nests are an incredible spongey dome, often built low down in a hedge. The birds weave together moss and cobwebs to build a cup-shaped wall, which gradually topples over to form the dome shape, and then they finish it off with lichen, which helps camouflage the nest. Afterwards, they line it (and sometimes adorn the entrance hole) with hundreds of feathers, which they pluck from dead birds.

Below ground, temperatures are slowly rising and fungal spores that colonised the ground the previous autumn are beginning to sprout. They send out thread-like hyphae, like masses of underground ribbons, which connect to plant and tree roots, linking them all together in an underground 'Wood Wide Web'. We only see the fruiting bodies (mushrooms) of these vast underground networks in autumn but for the rest of the year they are forming incredible symbiotic relationships with plants. These extraordinary networks exchange not only nutrients but also communications (see page 140).

THE KITCHEN

Cooking from the garden in April

Here are some crops that you might find in the kitchen garden this month: green garlic, asparagus, sorrel, purple sprouting broccoli, cauliflowers, chard, endive, lettuces, spring onions, radishes, spinach, turnips, cabbages, spring greens, rhubarb, parsley, chervil, coriander.

Ideas for eating from the garden this month
- Cavolo nero roasted in olive oil and salt until crisp at the edges, served topped with a tahini dressing and toasted pumpkin and sunflower seeds.
- Asparagus, steamed and dipped in soft-boiled eggs, alongside thick toast soldiers.
- Hot boiled potatoes tossed in sorrel leaves and butter, served with lamb cutlets.
- Leek and potato soup with croutons and wild garlic pesto, made by whizzing wild garlic with toasted hazelnuts, grated hard cheese, olive oil, lemon juice and salt.
- Pizza topped with white sauce, wilted chard, an egg and chunks of taleggio.

SNACK OF THE MONTH

Rhubarb and sheep's cheese *bolani* (stuffed Afghan flatbreads)

Eid al-Fitr, the Islamic celebration of the end of the fasting month of Ramadan, begins on the 9th at the sighting of the crescent moon. Eid is a huge feast, a great breaking of the fast, and *bolani* (stuffed savoury flatbreads) are among the traditional Eid recipes in Afghanistan. This version is made with a non-traditional, but delicious and very seasonal, filling: sweet leeks, tangy rhubarb, black onion seeds and salty, creamy cheese.

Makes 4 flatbreads

200g wholemeal flour, plus extra for kneading and rolling

1 teaspoon salt

6 tablespoons olive oil

1 large leek, trimmed, sliced and rinsed

1 teaspoon black onion seeds

1 teaspoon salt

pinch of chilli flakes

100g rhubarb, thinly sliced

1 garlic clove, thinly sliced

a handful of rocket, roughly chopped

100g soft sheep's milk cheese, crumbled (feta is also good)

Method

To make the dough, put the flour and salt in a bowl. Add 120ml tepid water and stir to bring the dough together. Turn it out on to a well-floured surface and knead for 5 minutes, or until the dough is smooth and elastic. Set aside under a clean tea towel for 20 minutes.

For the filling, heat 2 tablespoons of olive oil in a frying pan over a medium heat. Add the leeks, black onion seeds, salt

A

and chilli flakes and cook gently until soft and golden. Add the rhubarb and garlic and cook until the rhubarb is soft. Stir in the rocket to wilt for 30 seconds, then transfer the mixture to a bowl to cool slightly before stirring in the cheese.

Divide the dough into four equal pieces. On a well-floured surface, roll out each piece to a circle approximately 1mm thick. Place a tablespoon of the filling in the middle and spread it out to about 2cm from the edge. Fold all 4 sides into the middle to make a package, turn it over so that the joins are underneath, then gently roll it out again to increase the size a little, taking care not to press too hard and make the filling squeeze out.

Heat 1 tablespoon of olive oil in the frying pan over a medium heat and cook the first flatbread for 3 minutes on each side. Repeat with the other flatbreads, topping up with 1 tablespoon of olive oil for each one. Once they are all cooked, allow to cool for a few minutes before serving.

FOLK SONG

'English Country Garden'
Traditional, arr. Richard Barnard

You may well think you know this song, but this is an earlier version with a slightly different tune from that recorded in the 1960s by Jimmie Rodgers and the various cover versions that followed. This version is based on one of the earliest recordings of the song, sung by William Kimble in 1906 and collected by Cecil Sharp. Only the tune and the first line of lyrics exist, so the rest of the words have been written by composer Richard Barnard for this almanac. He has drawn on the lists of garden flowers and creatures found in later versions, focusing particularly on flowers seen in April gardens.

If you please now, won't you come with me
To my English country garden?
If you please now, won't you come with me
To my English country garden?

Daffodils and primrose, forget-me-nots and bluebells,
All underneath the blossom tree.
You will find all these flowers when you while away your
    hours
In an English country garden.

What will you see when you come away with me
To my English country garden?
What will you see when you come away with me
To my English country garden?

May

1 May Day (traditional)

1 Beltane, celebration of beginning of summer, cross-quarter day (Gaelic/Pagan)

1 International Workers' Day

5 International Dawn Chorus Day

5 Rogation Sunday/beating the bounds (Christian/traditional)

5 Orthodox Easter (Orthodox)

5 Cinco de Mayo

6 Early May bank holiday, England, Wales, Scotland. May Day bank holiday, Northern Ireland, Ireland

9 Ascension Day/Holy Thursday (Christian)

19 Whit Sunday/Pentecost (Christian)

26 Trinity Sunday (Christian)

27 Spring bank holiday, England, Wales, Scotland, Northern Ireland

30 Corpus Christi (Christian)

MAY IN THE GARDEN

The great green wave of May washes over the garden, the irresistible result of the meeting of light and warmth. Plant cells divide at pace, and unfurling, reaching, expanding photosynthesis is everywhere. In the soft May dawn, while the gardener sleeps, pea shoots twist up bamboo canes, climbing tendril over tendril. Ferns uncoil, oak leaves spread and twist themselves towards the light, grass stretches upwards. You could almost hear it, if it weren't for the overlapping choruses of birdsong ringing out across the early morning neighbourhood, blackbird over wren over chaffinch over warbler. They pronounce their eggs laid, these new lives coming, and guard them with song.

There is colour and flower, too, among the greenwood, a great display of bloom ready to be gathered up. Lilacs wave, foxgloves peek from shady corners, bluebells hang, tinkling their fairy bells, and tulips stand stately in terracotta pots. But white is May's second colour, the crests of its green wave. Elderflower and cow parsley, hydrangea and lily of the valley all bring a soft haze to the garden, and there is plenty of creamy blossom, too: apple, pear, plum and hawthorn, buzzy with pollinating bees.

On waking, the gardener might step barefoot, carefully, onto a dewy lawn freckled with daisies and dotted with fat golden dandelions, and add some more white to the garden: sheets, pegged along the line, to waft in the May Day sun. In the morning greenhouse, side shoots of tomato plants are pinched out, and the sharp green scent of the crushed foliage hits the nose, as green is curtailed here and energies concentrated there, all heading in one direction: fruit, and bounty.

The first small bounties are already emerging. Delicate fingertips are pricked as they grapple for the earliest, tiny sharp, green, tufted gooseberries, and then soothed as they slip broad beans from their soft, cushioned pods. The early crops of summer are here: the first peas popped into the mouth while the gardener stands, looking up at the Milk Moon.

Garden and weather folklore

The best-known of the May weather sayings is 'ne'er cast a clout till May be out'. A 'clout' was a piece of clothing, so it is obviously a suggestion that you shouldn't remove it, due to the weather being cold, but there is some disagreement about what the rest of the saying means. It could mean until the end of May but it could also refer to 'the may': hawthorn or may blossom. There are about half a million miles of hedgerows in the UK and the vast majority of them contain hawthorn, all of which bursts into white frothy flower in late April and early May. Bring on the may – but don't bring in the may, as it's considered unlucky to bring this blossom indoors.

Beware of the 'ice saints', as they were known throughout northern Europe. They are St Mamertus, St Pancras and St Servatius, whose feast days fall on 11th, 12th and 13th May respectively and who are supposed to bring winter's final blast of cold weather. In France they are the *les saints de glace*. They're known as *ledoví muži*, or ice men, in the Czech Republic, where they are joined by 'cold Sophia' on St Sophia's Day, 15th May. In Poland they are *zimni ogrodnicy*, the cold gardeners.

'St Urban gives the summer': St Urban's Day on 25th May is one of the (many) days in the year that are said to provide a prediction for the whole of the upcoming period.

In ancient Greece this was the time to eagerly look out for the heliacal rising of the Pleiades, the star cluster also known as the Seven Sisters. Heliacal rising is the moment a star first becomes visible above the eastern horizon pre-dawn, having been lost in the daytime sky, and it happens at roughly the same time annually. (This is a different phenomenon to the rising of the bright planets mentioned on page 152. These planets wander with more freedom across the sky, whereas the stars are fixed, though changing slowly over time.) For the ancient Greeks, the heliacal rising of the Pleiades in May heralded the beginning of the sailing season, an important date for a maritime society that used celestial navigation.

THE SEA

Average sea temperature in Celcius

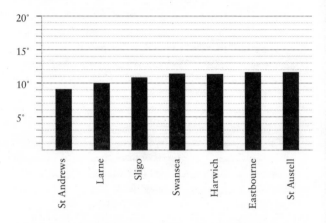

Spring and neap tides

Spring tides are the most extreme tides of the month, with
the highest rises and the lowest falls, and they follow a couple
of days after the full moon and new moon. These are the
times to choose a low tide and go rock-pooling, mudlarking
or coastal fossil-hunting. Neap tides are the least extreme,
with the smallest movement, and they fall in between the
spring tides.

Spring tides: 10th–12th and 24th–26th

Neap tides: 1st–3rd and 16th–18th

Spring tides are shaded in black in the chart opposite.

May tide timetable for Dover

For guidance on how to convert this for your local area, see page 8.

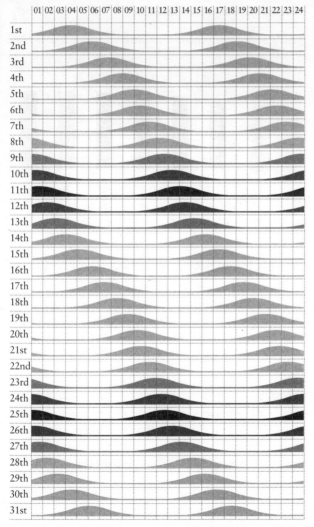

THE SKY

Stars, meteor showers and planets

Saturn returns as a morning star this month. It will be visible towards the end of the month from about 02.30, low in the southeast. Venus, Mars and Jupiter will still be unobservable.

31st: Brief view of Saturn and the moon. They will rise in the east at 02:30. They will get lost in the dawn at about 04.00 in the southeast at an altitude of 15 degrees.

The sun

20th: At solar noon (approximately 13.00 BST/IST) the sun will reach an altitude of 59 degrees in the London sky and 55 degrees in the Glasgow sky.

Sunrise and set
Coton in the Elms, Derbyshire

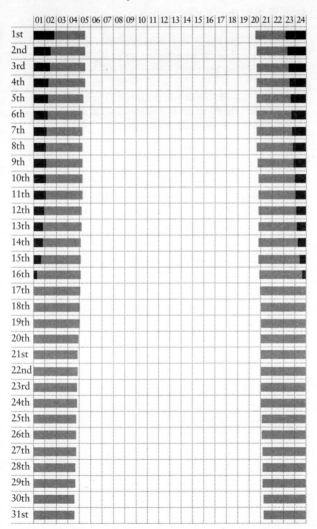

Moonrise and set

Like the sun, the moon rises roughly in the east and sets roughly in the west. It rises about 50 minutes later each day. Use the following guide to work out approximate moonrise times.

Full moon: Rises at around sunset time, but opposite the sun, so in the east as the sun sets in the west.
Last quarter: Rises at around midnight, and is at its highest point as the sun rises.
New moon: Rises at sunrise, in the same part of the sky as the sun, and so cannot be seen.
First quarter: Rises at around noon, and is at its highest point as the sun sets.

Moon phases

Last quarter – 1st May, 12.27

New moon – 8th May, 04.21

First quarter – 15th May, 12.48

Full moon – 23rd May, 14.53

Last quarter – 30th May, 18.12

The times given above are for the exact moment each moon phase occurs, for instance the moment that the moon is at its fullest.

May's full moon is known as the Mother's Moon, Milk Moon or Bright Moon.

Moon phases for May

1st	2nd	3rd	4th	5th
6th	7th	8th NEW	9th	10th
11th	12th	13th	14th	15th
16th	17th	18th	19th	20th
21st	22nd	23rd FULL	24th	25th
26th	27th	28th	29th	30th
31st				

M

MEDITATIONS

May's influences and guidance from Louise Press

The merry month of May is upon us…time to rejoice and dance barefoot in the grass! The sap is rising from the earth, bringing with it a verdancy to trees and hedgerows. The world seems to transform into Technicolor and all life is buzzing. The second Celtic fire festival of the year, Beltane on 1st May, celebrates fertility and the potency of the life force. It's a time of union, of love; a month to honour the blossoming of life.

Building on the foundations we've laid over the winter and early spring months, now is the time to make things happen; to use this potent growth period for realising our dreams. It's time to take action. Look around, be guided by the fruit trees and hedgerows this month. They are promising to bear fruit by adorning themselves in blossom. How will we show our promise this month?

The new moon in Taurus on 8th May will help to ground us. Along with all beings at this time, we feel the sap rising and love is in the air. Taurus brings a visceral, physical and embodied energy to our lives, and this new moon encourages us to be like the birds and bees; to lose ourselves in the pleasure of existing here and now in our physical bodies. Take a stroll outside, and you'll see that the rest of nature is having a party! The earth is singing, the sky is blue and we're in the middle of it all.

During the full moon in Sagittarius on the 23rd, our sense of creativity will be at its peak. Fun, focus and determination are the magical ingredients for this time of year. Do what we love and love what we do is the mantra. May is the month for walking our talk, getting into our stride. Are we in our flow? If not, now is the time to adjust. Take a few steps back and refocus. Are we being true to our winter dreaming or have we been hijacked by old patterns? We must be clear on our direction.

Making a space for May

Your nature table this month should be bursting with the colours of May – whites like the robes of the May Queen, bright greens like the young foliage, and pinks like the apple blossom, as well as ribbons and flowers in all colours. It will echo the beauty of the world outside the window.

Your table this month might include:
- Red, pink or white candles
- A vase of tulips and cow parsley
- A tiny pot of dandelion flowers and bluebells
- Coloured ribbons
- A little clump of moss or grass in a terracotta pot
- A stem of apple blossom, strung with ribbons

Light your candles for the Celtic fire festival of Beltane on 1st May, a celebration of early summer and all that the warmer months ahead will bring. Think on where we find ourselves: one of the most beautiful moments of the year.

M

GARDENS

Gardening by the moon

The following is a guide to gardening with the phases of the moon, according to traditional practices. For moon-gardening cynics it also works as a guide to the month's gardening if you disregard the exact dates.

Full moon to last quarter: 24th April–1st May (until 12.27) and 23rd (from 14.53)–30th May
A 'drawing down' energy. This phase is a good time for sowing and planting any crops that develop below ground: root crops, bulbs and perennials.
- Lift, split and replant daffodil clumps to revitalise them. Split and replant spring-flowering perennials.
- Direct sow beetroot, carrots, kohlrabi, radishes, spring onions, swedes and turnips.
- Plant summer-flowering bulbs and tubers: lilies, dahlias, gladioli.

Last quarter to new moon: 1st (from 12.27)–7th and 31st–6th June (until 13.37)
A dormant period, with low sap and poor growth. Do not sow or plant. A good time though for pruning, while sap is slowed. Weeding now will check growth well. Harvest any crops for storage. Fertilise and mulch the soil. Garden maintenance.
- Earth up potatoes.
- Prune spring-flowering clematis that has finished flowering.
- Tie in climbers and ramblers.
- Liquid feed clumps of bulbs that have finished flowering, to encourage more flowers next year.
- Put supports in place for herbaceous perennials so that they stay upright as they grow tall.
- Tie in sweet peas as they grow.
- Net fruit bushes to protect them from the birds.

New moon to first quarter: 8th–15th (until 12.48)

The waxing of the moon is associated with rising vitality and upward growth, above ground. Prepare for growth.

• Plant out vegetable plants, bedding plants and hanging baskets towards the end of the month, or once you are confident that frosts have passed.
• Direct sow lamb's lettuce, French beans, runner beans, sweetcorn, Brussels sprouts, calabrese, cauliflowers, Florence fennel, kale, lettuces, maincrop peas, spinach and purple sprouting broccoli, or wait until the next phase of the moon, which is even more conducive.
• Sow small amounts of herb seed in pots or seed trays indoors, or direct into the soil under cloches.
• The last month for sowing Brussels sprouts.
• Start cucumbers, courgettes, pumpkins and squashes in pots indoors to plant out next month.
• Pot chillies, tomatoes and any other vegetable plants that you are growing in containers into their final pots.

First quarter to full moon: 15th (from 12.48)–23rd (until 14.53)

The best time for sowing crops that develop above ground. Pot up or plant out seedlings and young plants. Take cuttings and make grafts but avoid all other pruning. Fertilise.

• Direct sow lamb's lettuce, French beans, runner beans, sweetcorn, Brussels sprouts, calabrese, cauliflowers, Florence fennel, kale, lettuces, maincrop peas, spinach and purple sprouting broccoli, plus cucumbers under cloches.
• Continue sowing small amounts of herb seed.
• Last month for sowing Brussels sprouts.
• Start cucumbers, courgettes, pumpkins and squashes in pots indoors for planting out next month.
• Plant out vegetable and bedding plants and hanging baskets towards the end of the month, or when you are confident that frosts have passed.

Note: Where no specific time for the change between phases is given, it happens outside of usual gardening hours. For exact changeover times for any late-night or pre-dawn gardening, refer to the May moon phase chart on page 108.

GARDEN CRAFT

Queen of the May crown

The Queen of the May traditionally headed May Day celebrations in towns and villages on May Day, dressed in white and wearing a crown of late spring and early summer flowers. Here are two ways to make your own.

For a wire crown with flowers and ribbons, you will need:
  Twine or floral tape
  Craft wire formed into a ring, or a wire wreath ring
  Flowers and foliage
  Ribbons in assorted colours

Tie the twine or attach one end of a length of floral tape to the wire wreath frame. Lay flowers and pieces of foliage along the frame and wind the twine or tape around to attach them. Keep doing this all the way around until it is covered, and go around again if you want a fuller effect. Tie differently coloured ribbons so that they stream down the wearer's hair at the back.

For a cardboard crown with flowers, you will need:
  Thin cardboard
  Tape
  Double-sided sticky tape

You can also turn making a May crown into a children's spring walk activity. Cut a wide band of cardboard to fit around the child's head, securing it with tape. Stick a band of double-sided sticky tape all around the outside. As you set off for the walk, remove the backing from the double-sided sticky tape and put the crown on the child's head. As they walk, encourage them to pick flowers and foliage and stick these to the tape to create their own May crown.

NATURE

Garden wildlife in May

Nights are noisy as this is the key time for mating hedgehogs, known as 'the rut'. Courtship can take hours, as males woo females by circling around, snorting and puffing. If you've ever witnessed this, you will know the females rarely look interested – it's astonishing hedgehogs manage to procreate at all. Not least because all the snorting and puffing attracts rival males who proceed to try their own luck, inevitably ending up in a fight. When mating does happen, it's a delicate affair – the female adopts a special body position with her spines flattened as the male mounts from behind. Contrary to what you might expect from observing this laborious ritual, hedgehogs may have several partners within a season.

The first brood of bumblebee offspring are all 'workers' (sterile females). Some will guard or clean the nest, while others will forage for nectar and pollen from flowers. Some of the nectar will be consumed by these bees, but most will be brought to the nest to feed other workers and the next batch of grubs. From now on, the queen will remain inside the nest, her main job now being to lay more eggs.

In the sky, summer migrants – including swifts, swallows and house martins – have arrived from the rainforests of the Congo, 6,500 kilometres away, and waste no time in preparing to breed. Males arrive a few days before the females to set up territories, and mating begins in earnest with the arrival of the females. By the month's end, every paired summer migrant that arrived earlier in the month will be sitting on eggs.

A female bird usually lays one egg a day, at dawn. Clutch size (the number of eggs per nest) depends on the species and food availability. Birds such as tits can have up to 14 eggs per brood. Swifts have three. For most garden birds, only after all the eggs are laid do the birds start brooding them, as this ensures all eggs hatch within a day of each other, so the chicks are easier to feed. Swifts are the exception and have chicks of different ages in the nest at the same time.

THE KITCHEN

Cooking from the garden in May

Here are some crops that you might find in the kitchen garden
this month: asparagus, broad beans, baby globe artichokes,
peas, radishes, wild rocket, beetroot, hispi cabbages,
cauliflowers, chard, endive, green garlic, lettuces, spring
onions, spinach, spring greens, turnips, sorrel, chives and
chive flowers, parsley, chervil.

Ideas for eating from the garden this month
- Hispi cabbage quartered, charred on the cut sides and
  roasted, then dressed with a soy and miso dressing and
  toasted sesame seeds.
- A spring-into-summer light stew of fried bacon pieces, broad
  beans, peas and chopped lettuce simmered in vegetable stock,
  served with thick hunks of bread and butter.
- A salad of baby potatoes roasted in their skins,
  charred asparagus and boiled eggs, dressed with salsa
  verde (parsley whizzed up with capers, anchovies, garlic,
  salt, olive oil and vinegar), and topped with broken-up
  chive flowers.
- Sautéed radishes piled on top of a thick piece of toast
  spread with cream cheese.
- Gooseberry pie, served with a jug of cream.

SNACK OF THE MONTH

Asparagus and Manchego *flautas* (stuffed corn tortillas)

Cinco de Mayo is a Mexican celebration commemorating the victory of Mexico over the French at the Battle of Puebla on 5th May 1862, and has become a celebration of Mexican-American culture, more popular in the US than in Mexico itself. It is treated as a day to eat Mexican food and drink lots of tequila! *Flautas* (stuffed corn tortillas) are among the traditional foods eaten on the day. They are usually stuffed with chicken and rolled into a cigar shape, then deep-fried or baked. Here is a seasonal asparagus and Manchego cheese version, which of course suits the shape very well, with a piquant tomato sauce to dip them in. While soft corn tortillas are traditional, soft wheat tortillas will work just as well if you can't find corn ones.

Makes 8

2 tablespoons olive oil, plus extra for frying

60g spring onions, trimmed and sliced diagonally

1 heaped teaspoon salt

1 teaspoon dried oregano

½ teaspoon ground cumin

a pinch of chilli flakes

200g asparagus, tough bottoms removed, cut in half

1 tablespoon white wine vinegar

2 tablespoons dry sherry

100g Manchego cheese, finely grated

30g flaked almonds

10g fresh coriander, roughly chopped

1 packet small soft tortilla wraps

M

For the sauce

400g tinned plum tomatoes
1 white onion, sliced
2 garlic cloves, sliced
½ teaspoon cayenne pepper
1 teaspoon salt
40g fresh coriander, roughly chopped
2 tablespoons olive oil

Method

For the sauce, put all the ingredients except the oil into a bowl and blend with a stick blender until smooth. Heat the oil in a pan, pour in the tomato mixture and cook over medium heat, stirring occasionally, until reduced by half and rich, about 20 minutes.

For the filling, heat the oil in a frying pan, add the spring onions, salt, oregano, cumin and chilli and cook for a minute or so over a medium heat. Add the asparagus stems, vinegar and sherry. Cover and simmer for 4 minutes, or until the asparagus has softened slightly. Lift out the asparagus stems and set aside, then transfer the rest of the mixture to a bowl and stir in the cheese, almonds and coriander.

Preheat the oven to 220°C, Gas Mark 7 and grease a baking tray. Heat a little oil in a frying pan and fry the tortilla wraps for a few seconds on each side to soften them. Place an asparagus stem down the middle of each tortilla and spoon some of the filling mixture over the top. Roll the tortilla up securely into a cigar shape and place it, seam side down, on the baking tray. Repeat with the rest of the tortillas, leaving space between them to allow them to crisp up. Bake for 15–20 minutes, or until golden. Once cool enough to handle, serve them with the sauce, which is good hot or cold.

FOLK SONG

'The Old Garden Gate'
Traditional, arr. Richard Barnard

A beautiful, sad song about a lover's inconstancy, told on
a May morning by the garden gate. This tune was a version
collected by Ralph Vaughan Williams in 1903. The lyrics are
mainly from an old Wiltshire version collected by Alfred
Williams in the early 1900s.

As I walked out one May morning
So early in the spring,
I placed my back against the old garden gate
For to hear my true love sing.

To hear my true love sing a song
And hear what he had to say,
For I wished to know more of his mind
Before he went away.

'Come sit you down all by my side,
On the grass that grows so green.
It's now past three quarters of a year
Since you and I together have been.'

'I will not come and sit down by you
Nor any other man,
Since you have been courting another girl
And your heart is no longer mine.'

I will never believe what an old man says
For his days they can't be long,
And I never believe what the young man says
For they promise but marry none.

There is a flower I've heard them say,
I wish that flower I'd find;
It's called heartsease by night and day
And would ease my troubled mind.

GARDEN SPECIAL

Summer nectar-rich plants

It is summer and everything is in flower, so you wouldn't think that insects would have any problem tracking down enough life-sustaining pollen. However, it all depends on what flowers they find. Many garden flowers have been subject to breeding that has lowered the amount of nectar and pollen they can offer, or that causes it to be hidden away. Roses are a great example of this, and in roses with many ruffles, the nectar and pollen are either non-existent or impossible for insects to reach. Choose simple types with open centres.

Dog rose, *Rosa canina*: The native dog rose, vigorous, with simple, open flowers. There are many other varieties that share this characteristic, so look around before you buy and plant.

Thyme, *Thymus vulgaris*: Covered in a great many small flowers that are very attractive to bees.

Lavender, *Lavandula angustifolia*: As soon as the purple flowers of lavender start to open, bees and other insects will be drinking the plentiful nectar. Plant as a path edging and your summer garden will be full of insects.

Hardy geranium, *Geranium*: Brilliant border plants that can flower all summer long. They have lovely simple, open flowers that bees love.

Buddleia, *Buddleja davidii*: Buddleia is not known as the 'butterfly bush' for nothing. On still, sunny days it will be covered in basking and supping butterflies.

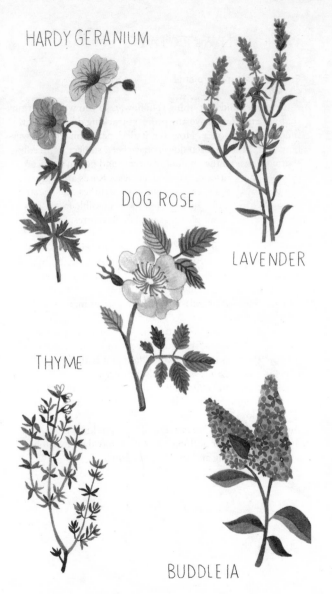

HARDY GERANIUM

LAVENDER

DOG ROSE

THYME

BUDDLEIA

June

1 Start of meteorological summer

1 Start of Pride Month

1 Start of Gypsy, Roma and Traveller History Month

3 June bank holiday, Ireland

7 7th–9th: Appleby Horse Fair – Romany and Traveller gathering

11 Shavuot/Feast of Weeks (Jewish), begins at sundown

11 14th–19th: Hajj – Islamic pilgrimage to Mecca

16 Father's Day

20 Summer solstice, at 21.50 – start of astronomical summer

20 Midsummer's Day

20 Litha (Pagan midsummer celebration)

21 World Humanist Day

24 St John's Day/traditional Midsummer's Day (Christian/traditional)

JUNE IN THE GARDEN

The gardener bruises mint between finger and thumb, releasing the scent of cool summer shade. Layers are finally shed, but a straw hat is pulled on against the solstice sun. Shoulders and nose are lightly burnt, freckles are forming, strawberries ripening. Pelargoniums bloom in coral, pink and red, ivy-leaved and trailing down walls – a Spanish courtyard transposed. Legs brush against Mexican daisies spilling from hot pathway cracks.

The garden is new and yet full, and like the sun itself is at the height of its powers. The roses know that there will never be a better moment, and they are everywhere – up walls, clambering over pergolas, and leaning out from borders offering their sweet, soft and cool petals. Cup in your hands and breathe in. They are queens of June despite the cacophony of all the other flowers taking their chance too. Verbascums and lupins, poppies and geraniums, alchemilla mollis and cosmos: all trip over themselves to fill the space with their blooms. And beneath the soft, undulating mounds of foliage, down in the shade, the weeds make a break for it, too. Unnoticed among all the glory, they can make some of their greatest gains now, pushing out across the warm soil, or down into its depths, or running to seed to scatter while the gardener is in raptures.

There's the snap and crunch of a runner bean, picked young and eaten raw, as well as a finger-sized courgette or three. Young carrots are pulled from the warm earth, as are the first of the new potatoes, small, sweet and waxy, to be eaten with handfuls of basil and dill. The last of the asparagus spears, too – a signal of the end of this waxing, expansive phase of summer. The meals almost make themselves, needing only a little heat, peppery olive oil and a lemon, cold wine and salt.

The boundary between day and night is loose, easy and expansive now that daylight is at its generous zenith. Day spills slowly into long, mauve, fragrant dusk, all fluttering moths, honeysuckle and Madonna lilies, with laughter floating across the gardens. Sunset comes late and dawn comes early; the two almost meet in the dreamy depths of the warm, twilit, midsummer night garden.

Garden and weather folklore

Midsummer's Day now hoves magically into view, and with it
a couple of pieces of weather-related lore. Until the change
from the Julian to the Gregorian calendar in 1752, when Britain
lost 11 days, St Barnabas Day (now on 11th June) fell on or
close to midsummer, as this traditional rhyme from the
mid-17th century attests:

> 'Barnaby bright, Barnaby bright,
> The longest day and the shortest night.
> When St Barnabas smiles both night and day,
> Poor ragged robin blooms in the hay.'

Ragged robin is a plant of old hay meadows, and the reference
to it here reminds us that weeds are still growing fast and often
flower in June. Haymaking was – and in many places still is –
one of the major jobs of the agricultural year, and timing was
crucial to ensure the hay was harvested while in peak condition
to keep for winter fodder. St Barnabas Day was traditionally the
first day of haymaking: 'On the day of St Barnabas, put the
scythe to the grass.'

The strength of the sun on Midsummer's Day was thought
to imbue herbs with healing qualities, and so this was the day
they were traditionally gathered, at dawn. Some would be dried
for later use in healing, but others were hung on the door to
ward off fairies and spirits, or were thrown on the midsummer
bonfire, which itself had magical properties.

Later, St John's Day, the 24th, became the traditional day to
celebrate midsummer. 'If the cuckoo sings after St John, the
harvest will be late.' The cuckoo – the harbinger of spring – is
supposed to start to sing on St Tiburtius' Day on 14th April
and stop singing on St John's Day. It makes sense therefore that
if it is still singing after midsummer, then the season is late and
so the harvest will be late, too.

THE SEA

Average sea temperature in Celcius

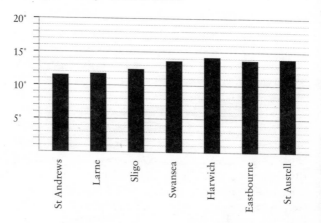

Spring and neap tides

Spring tides are the most extreme tides of the month, with the highest rises and the lowest falls, and they follow a couple of days after the full moon and new moon. These are the times to choose a low tide and go rock-pooling, mudlarking or coastal fossil-hunting. Neap tides are the least extreme, with the smallest movement, and they fall in between the spring tides.

Spring tides: 7th–9th and 23rd–25th

Neap tides: 14th–16th and 28th–30th

Spring tides are shaded in black in the chart opposite.

June tide timetable for Dover

For guidance on how to convert this for your local area, see page 8.

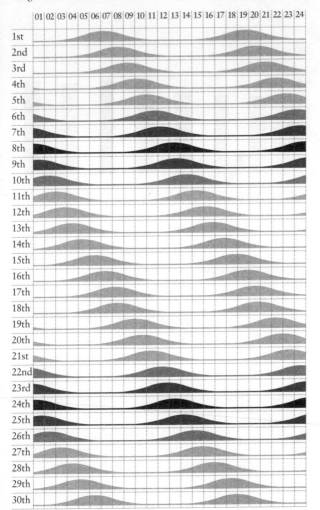

THE SKY

Stars, meteor showers and planets

This month a dim Mars will reappear briefly as a morning star at around 03.00 each day, low in the east. It will get lost in the dawn about an hour later. Saturn will get higher throughout the month but Venus and Jupiter will remain unobservable.

3rd: Brief view of Mars and the crescent moon. They will rise around 03.20 in the east and will get lost in the dawn at around 04.00 at an altitude of 12 degrees.

28th: Close approach of Saturn and the moon. They will rise in the east at around 01.00 and will be lost in the dawn by about 03.40 in the southeast at an altitude of 25 degrees.

The sun

20th: Summer solstice. The summer solstice falls at 21.50. This is the moment that the sun is above the Tropic of Cancer, the northernmost latitude at which it can be directly overhead. The word solstice comes from the Latin *solstitium*, meaning 'sun standing still', and is related to the position of sunset and sunrise on the horizon. Both points have been heading north day by day and will now appear to pause awhile, before setting off towards the south again.

20th: At solar noon (approximately 13.00 BST/IST) the sun will reach an altitude of 62 degrees in the London sky and 58 degrees in the Glasgow sky.

Sunrise and set
Coton in the Elms, Derbyshire

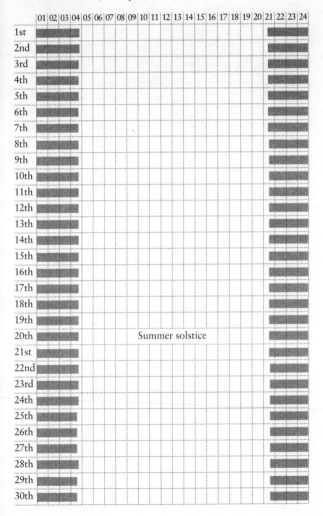

Summer solstice (20th)

Moonrise and set

Like the sun, the moon rises roughly in the east and sets roughly in the west. It rises about 50 minutes later each day. Use the following guide to work out approximate moonrise times.

Full moon: Rises at around sunset time, but opposite the sun, so in the east as the sun sets in the west.
Last quarter: Rises at around midnight, and is at its highest point as the sun rises.
New moon: Rises at sunrise, in the same part of the sky as the sun, and so cannot be seen.
First quarter: Rises at around noon, and is at its highest point as the sun sets.

Moon phases

New moon – 6th June, 13.37

First quarter – 14th June, 06.18

Full moon – 22nd June, 02.07

Last quarter – 28th June, 22.53

The times given above are for the exact moment each moon phase occurs, for instance the moment that the moon is at its fullest.

June's full moon is known as the Rose Moon, Flower Moon or Dyad Moon.

Moon phases for June.

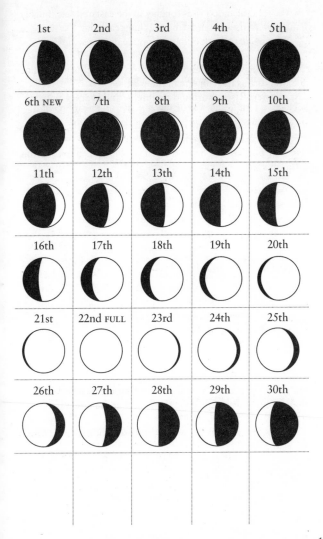

MEDITATIONS

June's influences and guidance from Louise Press

Now is the time to celebrate life and community; to fully embrace dreams that were seeded in winter, were protected and cared for in spring and are blooming into life this month. The sun reaches its zenith on the 20th, marked by the summer solstice, the standing still of the sun. This is the moment in the year when we experience the longest day and shortest night, celebrated as the Celtic festival of Litha, which means 'light'. Like the sun, we are at the peak of our expansive selves, and our actions are fuelled by these long, warm days of summer. June is the month for bold expression and creative freedom – the sky is the limit. However, there is a tendency at this time to overdo it. Being mindful of our boundaries and energy levels will serve us well. We can't fill from an empty cup, not even in the sunshine.

The Gemini new moon on 6th June invites us to consider our communication. Each new moon offers the opportunity to start again, to let go of what is no longer working for us and set new intentions for the lunar cycle ahead. This doesn't mean abandoning ideas, but suggests a reframe or change of perspective. How well are we communicating with our family, our friends and our wider community? This is the time to begin reaping the rewards of our efforts, so let's make sure we're shouting the correct message from the rooftops.

We'll get a massive boost from the June full moon in the grounded and determined sign of Capricorn on the 22nd. As much as new moons are about intention setting, full moons are a time for manifesting. They are powerful portals of self-discovery, and this Capricorn moon is no exception. We may feel an increased desire to succeed at this time, with clarity of action and solstice fire in our belly. We find ourselves at the halfway point in the year – this is 'make it happen' time. Energies are aligned to help us move obstacles, dig deep and find the courage to be our best selves and achieve our goals.

Making a space for June

Your June nature table can be full to bursting with the flowers of the moment: roses, lavender, herb Robert and campion, echoing old midsummer traditions of decorating doorways and windows with flowers.

Your table this month might include:
- A vase full of young oak leaves
- A jam jar of wild flowers
- Yellow and green candles
- A bowl of strawberries
- Colourful ribbons
- Lots of green and lots of colour

Midsummer was once a fire festival, and the Midsummer's Eve flame was thought precious and so was kept burning for as long as possible; long-burning stoves were extinguished and relit using it. Think of this as you light your candles on Midsummer's Eve – 19th June – remembering that we are now at the pinnacle of the year, the sun at its strongest.

GARDENS

Gardening by the moon

The following is a guide to gardening with the phases of the moon, according to traditional practices. For moon-gardening cynics it also works as a guide to the month's gardening if you disregard the exact dates.

Last quarter to new moon: 31st May–6th June (until 13.37) and 29th June–5th July

A dormant period, with low sap and poor growth. Do not sow or plant. A good time though for pruning, while sap is slowed. Weeding now will check growth well. Harvest any crops for storage. Fertilise the soil. Garden maintenance.

- Stop cropping asparagus on the summer solstice, 20th June, and allow the plants to grow tall and ferny. Water regularly with a balanced fertiliser.
- Net strawberries to protect them from birds.
- Earth up potatoes.
- Weed.
- Tie growing crops into supports.
- Inspect lilies for lily beetle and their larvae – they can strip the foliage in days.
- Deadhead roses as they fade, to encourage more flowers.

New moon to first quarter: 6th (from 13.37)–13th June

The waxing of the moon is associated with rising vitality and upward growth. Towards the end of this phase, plant and sow anything that develops crops above ground. Prepare for growth.

- Pot on chillies and tomatoes and any other vegetable plants that you are growing in containers into their final pots.
- Plant out bedding and hanging baskets, making sure to keep them well watered. Baskets will need watering every day.

First quarter to full moon: 14th–21st June

This is the best time for sowing crops that develop above ground, but is bad for root crops. Pot up or plant out seedlings

and young plants. Take cuttings and make grafts but avoid all
other pruning. Fertilise.

- Plant out bedding and hanging baskets, making sure to
  keep them well watered. Baskets will need watering
  every day.
- Place brassica collars around the stems to keep out cabbage
  root fly, and net them to keep out cabbage white butterflies.
- Plant sweetcorn in a block with the plants about
  35cm apart.
- Plant tomatoes into the ground or final pots in the
  greenhouse, with sturdy support. Nip out any side shoots
  on cordon varieties to keep them growing up a single stem.
  Feed weekly with a high potash fertiliser.
- Direct sow beetroot, carrots, courgettes, cucumbers, French
  and runner beans, kale, maincrop peas, swedes, turnips
  and herbs.
- Sow oriental leaves such as mizuna, mibuna, pak choi and
  mustard greens after the solstice.
- Feed everything.

Full moon to last quarter: 23rd–28th June

A 'drawing down' energy. This phase is a good time for sowing
and planting any crops that develop below ground: root crops,
bulbs and perennials.

- Sow 'maincrop' varieties of carrots for harvesting in
  autumn and winter. Also sow autumn beetroot, swedes,
  turnips and spring onions.
- Pot up strawberry runners to make new plants for next year.
- Lift, divide and replant overcrowded clumps of
  spring bulbs.

Note: Where no specific time for the change between phases is
mentioned, this is because it happens outside of usual
gardening hours. For exact changeover times for any late-night
or pre-dawn gardening, refer to the June moon phase chart on
page 132.

GARDEN CRAFT

Nature weaving

Weave midsummer flowers and foliage into a piece of nature art. You can do this on any scale you like, from a tiny miniature frame woven with daisies and ivy-leaved toadflax to a huge one featuring whole fern leaves and strips of cordyline.

You will need:
　　3 or 4 sticks to make a frame
　　String
　　Foliage and flowers
　　Feathers
　　Ribbons

First make your frame by placing the sticks on the ground and tying the ends together. If you can find a cleft stick you can skip this part as it will provide the framework. Next tie the string to one side and loop it backwards and forwards between two of the opposite sides, until you have lots of lines of string to weave in between. Tie this off at the end. Weave your foliage, flowers and feathers through the string. Enjoy it while it is fresh but you can also leave it to dry. The effect will be different but will be beautiful, too.

J

NATURE

Garden wildlife in June

Listen very carefully and you may just hear the hatching of an egg. Born naked and blind, bird chicks are entirely helpless. But their wide-open mouths are there for dropping insects, worms and caterpillars into, and it's not long before the chicks grow feathers and start to see, resembling the birds they actually are. Parent birds are using every second of daylight to keep their little ones fed. Letting aphids, caterpillars and other grubs remain on your garden plants means more food in the bellies of hungry chicks.

Leafcutter bees are on the wing now. Like red mason bees, they nest in cavities and will use bee 'hotels'. However, instead of using mud to line their nests they use leaves, which they roll together like cigars, to form a series of walled cells, each containing one bee grub and its little parcel of food. Look out for bees carving the perfect elliptical shapes into the leaves of roses, wisteria, beech and Eastern redbud. You may be lucky enough to have them nesting in your garden.

Hedgehogs are still mating, though many females will be pregnant by now. Gestation lasts for around four weeks, during which time the female will find and prepare a nest, typically at the base of a hedge, among thick brambles, in a compost heap or under a shed. She will gather mosses, grass, leaves and other garden debris to make it snug.

Below ground, the invisible fungal networks are busy. Mycorrhizal fungi can't make its own food, so it feeds from the roots of plants. As their ribbon-like hyphae spread out further than tree roots can, they have access to more nutrients in the soil, which they pass back to the plant roots. The sharing of information between trees and other plants via these underground fungal networks is also invaluable to the trees and plants – if one tree is attacked by a pest, other trees in the area can release chemical compounds that attract the pest's predators, for the good of the whole community.

THE KITCHEN

Cooking from the garden in June

Here are some crops that you might find in the kitchen garden
this month: globe artichokes, asparagus, carrots, courgettes
(and their flowers), broad beans, cauliflowers, chard, endive,
lettuces, spring greens, spring onions, new potatoes, radishes,
wild rocket, spinach, beetroot, garlic, peas, turnips, chives,
basil, mint, dill, marjoram, thyme, oregano, gooseberries,
strawberries, blackcurrants, cherries, raspberries, redcurrants,
rhubarb.

Ideas for eating from the garden this month

- Courgette flowers, centres removed, dipped in batter and
  fried, served with a wedge of lemon.
- Salad niçoise – boiled new potatoes with green beans,
  lettuce, tomatoes, olives and tuna.
- Double-podded broad beans, mashed into a rough purée,
  spread on bread and topped with crumbled feta, chopped
  mint and olive oil.
- An 'Eton mess' of gently poached, sweetened
  blackcurrants, whipped cream and crushed meringue.
- Gin, infused with chopped cucumber overnight, served
  with cold tonic and a splash of elderflower cordial.

J

SNACK OF THE MONTH

Ham, watercress and turnip *croquetas*

At midnight on 23rd June, the eve of the feast of San Juan (St John the Baptist), a cannon booms and the Andalusian village of Lanjarón erupts with water. The town's *Fiestas del Agua y del Jamón* (festival of water and ham) begins, its spring-fed fountains flow, and hundreds of people take to the streets with waster pistols, buckets and hoses. The aim is to soak everyone you meet. At 1.00am the cannon booms again and the ham part of the fiesta begins, with slice after slice of local ham and gallons of wine. Jamón *croquetas* (ham croquettes) are a traditional Spanish tapas dish. Both watercress and turnips are in season at this time, and although they are not traditional, their peppery nature compliments the rich saltiness of the ham.

Makes about 12 *croquetas*
30g butter
30ml olive oil, plus extra to oil the bowl
1 large red onion, finely diced
1 small turnip, finely diced
1 pinch freshly grated nutmeg
1 tablespoon salt
1 teaspoon ground black pepper
100g Serrano ham (or any other dry-cured ham), finely diced
80g plain flour, plus extra for coating the *croquetas*
450ml milk
2 large handfuls of watercress, roughly chopped
2 eggs, beaten
200g panko breadcrumbs
rapeseed oil, for deep frying

Method

Heat the butter and oil in a pan, add the onion and turnip and cook over a medium–low heat for about 5 minutes, until starting to colour. Add the nutmeg, salt, pepper and ham and continue to fry for a minute. Add the flour and cook, stirring continuously, until starting to brown.

After a few minutes, start adding the milk little by little, stirring well each time with a whisk or wooden spoon to make a smooth paste. You are aiming for a thick béchamel sauce. Once all the milk has been added, stir in the chopped watercress and leave to cool in the pan. Decant into a lightly oiled bowl, cover with clingfilm and chill for at least 6 hours in the refrigerator or, even better, overnight, so that it firms up and makes handling a little easier.

Put a thick layer of flour on one plate, the beaten eggs in a shallow bowl and the breadcrumbs on another plate. Spoon a tablespoonful of the thick béchamel into the flour and shape it in to a slightly oval ball, coating it with flour. Then dip it in the egg to coat, then finish by coating it with breadcrumbs. Repeat with the rest of the mixture.

Fill a pan or deep-fryer one-third full with oil and heat it to 180°C, or until a cube of bread dropped into it turns golden brown in 15 seconds. Fry the *croquetas* one or two at a time until deep golden, turning them over to ensure they colour evenly. Lift them onto a plate lined with kitchen paper to drain and cool slightly, then serve hot.

J

FOLK SONG

'The Seeds of Love'
Traditional, arr. Richard Barnard

This is one of the first songs ever collected by celebrated folk song collector Cecil Sharp. He heard it one morning in 1903, sung softly by gardener John England as he mowed the lawn.

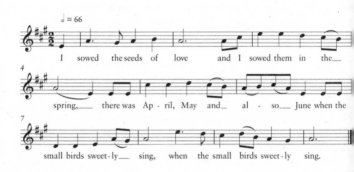

I sowed the seeds of love
And I sowed them in the spring,
There was April, May and also June
When the small birds sweetly sing,
When the small birds sweetly sing.

My garden it was full
With seeds of every kind,
But I had not freedom for to choose
The flower that was on my mind,
O, the flower that was on my mind.

My gardener he stood by,
So I asked him to choose for me
And he chose the violet, lily and the pink,
But I did refuse all three,
But I did refuse all three.

The lily I forsook
Because it fades too soon,
And the pink and violet I did overlook,
So I vowed I'd wait till June,
So I vowed I'd wait till June.

In June there is the rose
And that is the flower for me,
But I've often plucked at the red rose bush
And have gained but a willow tree,
And have gained but a willow tree.

O, the willow tree will twist,
And the willow tree will twine,
And I wish I was back in that young girl's arms
That held this heart of mine,
That held this heart of mine.

July

6 Al Hijra/Islamic New Year, start of the Islamic year 1446, begins at sighting of the crescent moon

12 Battle of the Boyne, bank holiday Northern Ireland

13 Wimbledon Women's Singles Final

14 Wimbledon Men's Singles Final

14 UEFA Euro 2024 Final, Olympiastadion Berlin

15 St Swithin's Day (Christian/traditional)

23 Birthday of Haile Selassie (Rastafarian)

26 2024 Summer Olympics Opening Ceremony, River Seine, Paris

JULY IN THE GARDEN

Tall grasses come up to meet the palm. The wrist twists and trailing fingers brush through grass heads, releasing pollen and moths and a cloud of midges to dance in the hot afternoon sun. This is the first of the waning months in the garden, but there is heat, and with it sometimes come thunderstorms – fat droplets falling on the green growth – and sometimes drought, the countryside turning golden before its time. Either way there is a maturing this month, with giddy midsummer behind us. The trees are a deeper green now, the canopy closing, only the very tips of the trees having full access to sunlight. They wave in the breeze, against blue skies: the winners.

July is a quiet month – the flurry and blossom extravaganza of spring and early summer are past, the fruits of autumn yet to come. We are in between, and even the birds have fallen silent, their eggs laid and hatched. Now the work is in fetching and feeding and raising, not singing about it. Tight green blackberries, dense sharp little apples, still to swell, and hazelnuts embryonic in their pale papery wraps – serious work is being undertaken by the plant world. The long hours of sunlight are being utilised in the plants' bids for immortality, the making of potential descendants, packaged into seed and fruit.

All very well, thinks the gardener, where plums and apples and blue tits are concerned. In the flower border, though, gardeners take it on themselves to stall this moment. They move around the garden with scissors, snipping off the fading flowers with one hand, and holding a soft, crumpled mess of spent flowers – cornflower, marigold, cosmos, rose – in the other. The gardener sends a signal down the stem of the plant: 'Try again, try again, one more flower, this time…' Making the most of the plant's desire to procreate, they draw out the season by misdirection. In the warm evenings, under the Mead Moon, they fill their watering cans and tip in seaweed fertiliser, swirling darkly in the cold, tinny depths, then water it onto parched and greedy roots. All the better to keep the flowers flowing through the dog days, and to extend hot and humid high summer.

Garden and weather folklore

The most famous piece of weather lore for July – perhaps even for the whole year – relates to St Swithin's Day:

> *'St Swithin's Day if thou dost rain, for 40 days it will*
> *   remain,*
> *St Swithin's Day if thou be fair, for 40 days will rain*
> *   na mair.'*

Although it doesn't hold that one day can foretell forty more, there is some truth behind this saying. Over high summer our weather tends to lock into a pattern, so whatever that is by the 15th July is likely to continue right up until late August, when autumnal weather begins. Incidentally, rain on St Swithin's blesses the apples and ensures an excellent harvest in autumn.

Some weather lore that has persisted for thousands of years is the idea of the 'dog days', the hottest, muggiest days of summer, between mid-July and mid-August. The name comes from the heliacal rising of Sirius, the Dog Star and the brightest star in the sky. Heliacal rising is the moment a star first becomes visible above the eastern horizon pre-dawn, having been lost in the daytime sky, and happens at roughly the same time annually (a different phenomenon to the rising of the bright planets mentioned on page 152, as planets wander across the sky, while the stars are relatively fixed, their timings slipping slowly over time). Sirius's heliacal rising can now be observed in the eastern pre-dawn sky from around 21 August. In ancient Egypt, Sirius's heliacal rising occurred in early July and signalled the Nile would soon flood. In ancient Greece and Rome, it was thought to be a time of bad tempers, bad luck and general unrest due to the stultifying heat. However, in Britain and Ireland it has been seen as a time to wish for dry weather for the harvest:

> *'Dog days bright and clear indicate a happy year*
> *But when accompanied by rain, for better times our hopes*
> *   are in vain.'*

THE SEA

Average sea temperature in Celcius

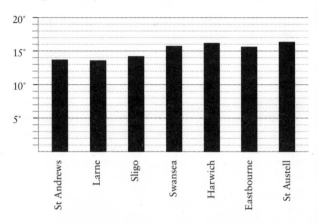

Spring and neap tides

Spring tides are the most extreme tides of the month, with the highest rises and the lowest falls, and they follow a couple of days after the full moon and new moon. These are the times to choose a low tide and go rock-pooling, mudlarking or coastal fossil-hunting. Neap tides are the least extreme, with the smallest movement, and they fall in between the spring tides.

Spring tides: 6th–8th and 22nd–24th

Neap tides: 14th–16th and 29th–31st

Spring tides are shaded in black in the chart opposite.

July tide timetable for Dover

For guidance on how to convert this for your local area, see page 8.

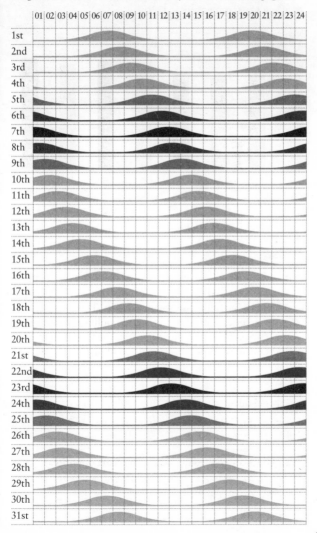

THE SKY

Stars, meteor showers and planets

A few of the bright planets, having been well hidden close to the sun most of the year, come out to play this month, though unfortunately at times most of us are in our beds. This month Mars and Jupiter will be visible for a few hours in the early hours. Saturn will rise in the east at before midnight and will get lost in the dawn, at an altitude of 30 degrees, at around 04.00 in the south.

2nd: Close approach of Mars and the crescent moon. They will rise in the northeast at around 02.00 and will become lost in the dawn at around 04.00 at an altitude of 20 degrees.
23rd–24th: Close approach of Saturn and the moon. They will rise at around 23.00 in the east and reach an altitude of 33 degrees before becoming lost in the dawn in the south the next day.
30th: Close approach of Mars and the moon. They will rise at around 01.00 in the northeast and reach 40 degrees altitude in the east before becoming lost in the dawn at around 04.40.
31st: Brief close approach of the moon and Jupiter. They will rise at around 01.30 in the northeast and reach 40 degrees altitude in the east before becoming lost in the dawn at around 04.30.

The sun

5th: Aphelion. This is the moment in the year when the earth is furthest from the sun in its imperfect orbit. At 06.06 the sun will be 152,099,968 kilometres away (compare with perihelion on 3rd January, see page 16).
20th: At solar noon (approximately 13.00 BST/IST) the sun will reach an altitude of 59 degrees in the London sky and 50 degrees in the Glasgow sky.

Sunrise and set
Coton in the Elms, Derbyshire

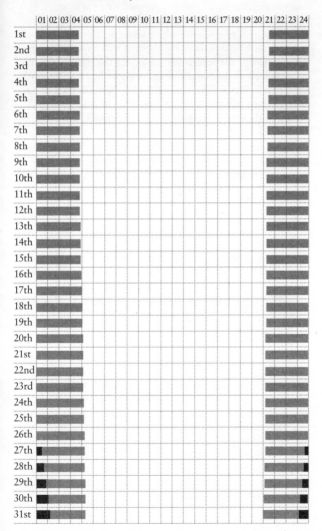

Moonrise and set

Like the sun, the moon rises roughly in the east and sets roughly in the west. It rises about 50 minutes later each day. Use the following guide to work out approximate moonrise times.

Full moon: Rises at around sunset time, but opposite the sun, so in the east as the sun sets in the west.
Last quarter: Rises at around midnight, and is at its highest point as the sun rises.
New moon: Rises at sunrise, in the same part of the sky as the sun, and so cannot be seen.
First quarter: Rises at around noon, and is at its highest point as the sun sets.

Moon phases

New moon – 5th July, 23.57

First quarter – 13th July, 23.49

Full moon – 21st July, 11.17

Last quarter – 28th July, 03.51

The times given above are for the exact moment each moon phase occurs, for instance the moment that the moon is at its fullest.

July's full moon is known as the Hay Moon, Wyrt Moon or Mead Moon.

Moon phases for July

1st	2nd	3rd	4th	5th NEW
6th	7th	8th	9th	10th
11th	12th	13th	14th	15th
16th	17th	18th	19th	20th
21st FULL	22nd	23rd	24th	25th
26th	27th	28th	29th	30th
31st				

J

MEDITATIONS

July's influences and guidance from Louise Press

There is a stillness to July. The peak of energy we felt in June is beginning to wane and the world around us seems to pause. Resourced and energised by the season, we're able to kick back a little and enjoy the fruits of our labour. The outdoors is calling us and nature is inviting connection. For a moment, let's cast our minds back to February when we tuned into our senses: how different it feels today. Look up and see the birds cruise the thermals. Listen to the laughter in the air and feel the cool breeze against our skin under a welcome canopy of shade. As quick bursts of summer rain drench the dry earth, smell the unmistakable scent of petrichor (the pleasantly earthy smell of rain on dry soil).

On the 5th, our new moon is in the sign of Cancer. Emotional and protective, the energies around this time will be inward-looking. These are the darkest nights of the lunar cycle, with little sign of the moon in the sky to light our way. However, we see much more in the dark than we think. As the light around us dims, our inner spark kindles and we are guided by our intuition. The high-summer energies are sometimes overwhelming, so this new moon can bring relief as it calls us to retreat into our shell; to seek safe haven and tune into our inner wisdom. This is where the treasure is to be found.

On the 21st we are coaxed out of our shells by the loyal and patient Capricorn full moon. What a difference a fortnight can make in the way we feel. Illuminated by the full power of the manifesting moon, we are encouraged to emerge into the light, sure-footed and focused. Our new moon retreat has gifted us a little summer dream time, perhaps showing us what is holding us back from fully shining our light. Capricorn draws out these elements and brings us face to face with often self-imposed obstacles. This full moon can show us how to clear the way. Remember your lightness of being; Capricorn energies can sometimes be a little serious.

Making a space for July

One of the old names for July's full moon was the 'Wyrt Moon', named after 'wyrts', or healing plants, as this is the time that many leafy herbs are at their best. Make the most of this on your nature table with little pots of herbs or with stems of mint and oregano to waft the scents of July through the house.

Your table this month might include:
- Dark green candles
- Lots of green foliage
- A pot of basil or mint – pot it up into a small terracotta pot to make it look pretty
- A jam jar of wild flowers, or a dried bunch – it is haymaking time
- Shells
- Silver birch bark

At the beginning of the month, consider writing a word or intention for the month ahead, and tucking it under a stone or a pot on your table. Revisit it at the end of the month. Light your candles even though the evenings are still light. Take some time to think about the gentle waning of summer and the subtle but important ways in which the contents and character of your nature table have changed over the past two months.

GARDENS

Gardening by the moon

The following is a guide to gardening with the phases of the moon, according to traditional practices. For moon-gardening cynics it also works as a guide to the month's gardening if you disregard the exact dates.

Last quarter to new moon: 29th June–5th July and 28th July–4th August (until 12.13)

A dormant period, with low sap and poor growth. Do not sow or plant. A good time though for pruning, while sap is slowed. Weeding now will check growth well. Harvest any crops for storage. Fertilise the soil. Garden maintenance.

- Apples and pears set many more fruits than they can bring to maturity. Thin out the young fruits. Thin out grape bunches.
- Pinch out the side shoots on tomatoes and continue to feed regularly with a high potash feed and to tie the stems in.
- Pinch out the tops of climbing beans when they reach the tops of their frames.
- Harvest onions, garlic and shallots for storage during this 'dormant' period if you can.
- Weed regularly.
- Earth up potatoes.
- Prune cherries and plums if they need pruning.
- Once summer raspberries have finished fruiting, cut the fruited canes to the ground and tie in this year's new growths.

New moon to first quarter: 6th–13th July

The waxing of the moon is associated with rising vitality and upward growth. Towards the end of this phase, plant and sow anything that develops crops above ground. Prepare for growth.

- Also towards the end of this phase, sow, plant out or take cuttings of all of those things mentioned in the first quarter to full moon phase.

First quarter to full moon: 14th–21st July (until 11.17)

This is the best time for sowing crops that develop above ground, but is bad for root crops. Pot up or plant out seedlings and young plants. Take cuttings and make grafts but avoid all other pruning. Fertilise.

- Last chance to sow French beans and maincrop peas for autumn harvesting.
- Plant out winter brassicas and protect with netting to keep off cabbage white butterflies.
- Sow salad leaves for autumn and winter harvesting: mustard greens, mizuna, mibuna, pak choi and chop suey greens, as well as kale, rocket, lettuce and Swiss chard.
- Take cuttings of woody herbs such as rosemary, sage and thyme.
- Feed everything.

Full moon to last quarter: 21st (from 11.17)–27th July

A 'drawing down' energy. This phase is a good time for sowing and planting any crops that develop below ground: root crops, bulbs and perennials.

- Sow beetroot for autumn harvesting. Continue to sow late maincrop carrot and turnip varieties and spring onions.
- Plant out leeks.
- Pot up strawberry runners to make new plants to plant out next year.

Note: Where no specific time for the change between phases is mentioned, this is because it happens outside of usual gardening hours. For exact changeover times for any late-night or pre-dawn gardening, refer to the July moon phase chart on page 154.

GARDEN CRAFT

Pressing flowers

Now that the garden is full of flowers, collect some up and press them. Once pressed, they can be made into a memento of this moment in the year – date a piece of thick paper and stick the flowers to it with tiny pieces of brown paper parcel tape, then write the names of each plant next to it. Do this at intervals throughout the year for a reminder of your garden. Or save up the pressed flowers and make them into cards or bookmarks.

You will need:
    Heavy books
    Newspaper
    Kitchen paper
    Flowers from the garden

Open a large book and place a piece of newspaper and a piece of kitchen paper on it. Arrange your flowers on the kitchen paper, not touching each other, and as flat as possible. Place another piece of kitchen paper over it, and another piece of newspaper. You can do this several times within the same book. Once it is all loaded up, top it with several other heavy books. Leave for about three weeks and then carefully remove your pressed flowers.

J

NATURE

Garden wildlife in July

The garden takes on a new role this month as nestlings join the jostle for food and water at feeding stations and in trees and borders. These are perilous times for baby birds, for whom predators, such as larger birds, cats and foxes, lie in wait. Many fledglings are not quite as grown as perhaps they would like. Most are still unable to fly, and their parents leave them under a hedge or in a similar sheltered spot, where they will continue to feed them while teaching them to find their own food.

Many garden butterflies are on the wing from the end of the month, including colourful favourites such as the peacock, red admiral, small tortoiseshell and comma. These are fresh new adults hatched from eggs laid in spring. Feeding from nectar-rich plants like buddleia, oregano, *Verbena bonariensis* and Shasta daisies, they will mate and lay eggs of a second brood, whose caterpillars can be found on nettles between now and September. Adults from the second brood will then hibernate (or, in the case of the red admiral, may fly south for winter), emerging in spring to mate and start the whole process off all over again.

This is another exciting time of year for garden ponds, as thousands of tiny frogs, toads and newts (known as efts) are leaving the water, while dragonflies and damselflies mate and lay eggs. You may spot male dragonflies resting on a 'perch', from which they defend their territory against rival males. They also hunt from this perch and return with their prey, to eat it.

Hedgehogs will now be having their first litters, giving birth to up to seven hoglets, which are born bald and blind. The mother will continue to forage for food and water for herself – sometimes during the day – and will return to feed milk to her young while they are too small to leave the nest.

Far above, swift chicks are getting ready for the long flight to the Congo, doing press-ups with their wings. Towards the end of the month, they will join their parents in screaming parties racing around the rooftops, before disappearing south.

THE KITCHEN

Cooking from the garden in July

Here are some crops that you might find in the kitchen garden this month: French beans, runner beans, broad beans, courgettes (and their flowers), cucumbers, globe artichokes, peas, fennel, shallots, rhubarb, beetroot, endive, garlic, lettuces, spring onions, new potatoes, radishes, wild rocket, baby turnips, mint, basil, dill, chives, marjoram, thyme, oregano, calendula flowers, blackcurrants, gooseberries, loganberries, raspberries, cherries, blueberries.

Ideas for eating from the garden this month
- Very small courgettes and their flowers, chopped raw into a salad with watercress, goats' cheese and mint.
- Globe artichokes boiled and their leaves removed one by one, then dipped into melted salted butter.
- Fennel, blanched then roasted in butter until caramelised, with buffalo mozzarella and chopped toasted almonds.
- Cherries cooked in a splash of water and spoonful of sugar until syrupy, served warm with vanilla ice cream and amaretti biscuits.
- Ricotta and raspberries wrapped in fig leaves and baked on the barbecue, then honey drizzled over.

J

SNACK OF THE MONTH

Kartoffelpuffer (potato pancakes) with sweet potato, apple and Cheddar sauce

A classic German snack to eat alongside a glass of *weissbier* for the Euro 2024 final. Traditionally, these are made of grated potato, nutmeg and sometimes onion. Here, they also contain chopped gherkins and dill. Serve them with traditional apple sauce for dipping, which cuts the fattiness beautifully, or with this sweet potato, apple and Cheddar sauce, which is a gorgeous balance of sweet and savoury.

Makes about 16 pancakes

For the sauce

1 large cooking apple, peeled and cut into cubes

1 small sweet potato, peeled and cut into cubes

1 garlic clove, crushed

1 teaspoon salt

½ teaspoon ground cinnamon

40g Cheddar cheese, finely grated

For the potato pancakes

400g waxy potatoes, peeled

2 small onions

2 large eggs, lightly beaten

100g plain flour

1 heaped teaspoon salt

½ teaspoon finely ground black pepper

2 teaspoons Dijon mustard

20g fresh dill, finely chopped

60g gherkins, finely diced

60ml rapeseed oil

Method

To make the sauce, put the apple and sweet potato in a pan with the garlic, salt, cinnamon and 150ml water. Cover, bring to a simmer, then turn the heat down and allow to simmer away for 20 minutes. Check halfway through just in case the water has evaporated, and add a dash more if needed. Once soft, mash until smooth and stir in the cheese.

To make the pancakes, grate the potatoes and onion into a bowl. Tip the mixture into a clean tea towel, gather it up and squeeze out as much liquid as possible. Discard the liquid, then return the potato and onion mixture to the bowl.

Add the eggs, flour, salt, pepper, mustard, dill and gherkins into the potato mix and stir to combine. Pour the oil into a frying pan and heat until hot. Take a heaped tablespoon of the potato mixture and carefully place in the oil, patting it down to flatten it slightly. Cook for about 3 minutes or until well browned and crispy at the edges, then turn and repeat on the other side. Lift onto a plate lined with kitchen paper to drain and repeat with the rest of the mixture. Allow the pancakes to cool briefly, then serve with the sauce to dip.

J

FOLK SONG

'Cupid's Garden'

Traditional, arr. Richard Barnard

This song is thought to have been written about Cuper's Gardens, a 17th–18th-century pleasure garden on the south side of the Thames in London. It was dubbed 'Cupid's Gardens', for perhaps obvious reasons, and it closed in 1760 after losing its licence because of a problem with pickpockets. This version of the song is taken from a singer heard by Cecil Sharp in Taunton in 1904 and lyrics published in the 1890s and 1900s.

As down in Cupid's Garden with pleasure I did go
To see the fairest flowers that in the garden grow.
The first it was the jasmine, then lily, pink and rose;
They are the finest flowers that in the garden grow,
That in the garden grow.

I'd not been in the garden but scarcely half an hour
When I saw two maidens beneath a shady bower,
And one it was sweet Nancy, so beautiful and fair,
The other was a virgin and did the laurel wear,
And did the laurel wear.

I boldly stepped up to them and unto them did say,
'Are you engaged already, come tell to me, I pray?'
'No, I am not yet promised, I solemnly declare;
I mean to stay a virgin and still the laurels wear,
And still the laurels wear.'

So, hand in hand together this loving couple went,
To know the fair maid's mind, it was my sole intent.
I asked if she would slight me while I to sea did go.
She answered me, 'Not I, sir, I love my sailor bold,
I love my sailor bold.'

It's down in Portsmouth Harbour, my ship lies waiting
      there;
And I must go to sea, dear, when winds they do blow fair,
And if I should return here how happy I should be
With you, my love, my true love sat smiling on my knee,
Sat smiling on my knee.

August

- **1** Lammas (Christian) – blessing of the First Fruits of harvest festival

- **1** Lughnasadh, celebration of the beginning of autumn and the harvest, cross-quarter day (Gaelic/Pagan)

- **5** Summer bank holiday, Scotland. August bank holiday, Ireland

- **11** 2024 Summer Olympics Closing Ceremony, Stade de France, Paris

- **12** Tisha B'Av/Jewish day of mourning, begins at sundown

- **15** The Assumption of Mary (Christian)

- **25** 25th–26th: Notting Hill Carnival, London

- **26** Summer bank holiday, England, Wales, Northern Ireland

- **26** Krishna Janmashtami – Krishna's birthday (Hindu)

- **28** 2024 Summer Paralympics Opening Ceremony, Champs-Élysées and Place de la Concorde, Paris

AUGUST IN THE GARDEN

An early morning haze, burned off by the Lammas sun. Feet on the hot terrace. A blanket thrown on the lawn. Clouds drifting in a blue sky above. Vivid violet pinpricks of Verbena bonariensis floating above the garden borders, alongside fat, layered dahlias; towering, golden sunflowers; zinnias in their Mexican fiesta colours; acid yellow dill flowers; crazy love-in-a-mist seed heads. And the gardener has stopped battling – the garden is now all that it will be.

It is time for the first harvest celebration. The vegetable garden overflows with summer ripening, and has become a market place for languid browsing and plucking. Hmmm… beetroot and blackberries? Courgette and dill? Florence fennel and raspberries? The trug runneth over, a cornucopia. The gardener lays the outdoor table. A plate of greenhouse-warmed beefsteak tomatoes, sliced and salted and touched with olive oil. A tearable loaf and a young cheese. A bowl of plums. The swifts make their final swoops of the year overhead, their victory laps, for having completed their work here. They've raised their babies and will leave soon, escaping encroaching autumn. Their screeching cries are gradually replaced by the steady beat of crickets in the long grass.

The garden has become lazy, the pertness of early summer replaced by a languid, slightly spent air. Stems flop over paths, leaves are nibbled and imperfect, and everywhere there is the fading glamour of flower heads running to seed.

It is a transitional moment, because as summer fades, intimations of autumn steal in, unwanted as they may be yet. In this final summer month, the garden takes on a honeyed edge of gold. Grasses are buff and the yellowing of leaf edges hints at what is to come. Berries are starting to fill out and take on a slight burnish, hanging heavy from the trees and bushes. And the spiders have begun to appear, too, strung between poppy seed heads and gates, where they wait patiently for their season to begin.

Garden and weather folklore

St Bartholomew's Day on the 24th is the most important
day in August weather lore, falling as it does 40 days after
St Swithin's Day. It is another day that is supposed to set the
weather for the coming period, and it gives some considerable
hope if the summer has been wet. 'All the tears that St Swithin
can cry St Bartelmy's mantle will wipe dry' – a dry autumn
will follow a wet summer. St Bartholomew has his finger in all
sorts of harvest-time pies, too. 'On St Bartholomew's Day
take the honey away' – it is time to collect summer honey
from the beehives – and 'Rain at St Bartholomew's tide
christens the potatoes'.

As we reach the end of summer, minds inevitably turn to
winter, and how harsh or otherwise it might be. Count the
fogs in August, and that will tell you how many snowfalls the
winter will bring, while a dry first week of August brings a
harsh winter.

A

THE SEA

Average sea temperature in Celcius

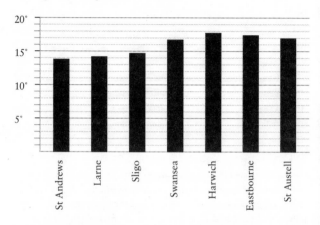

Spring and neap tides

Spring tides are the most extreme tides of the month, with the highest rises and the lowest falls, and they follow a couple of days after the full moon and new moon. These are the times to choose a low tide and go rock-pooling, mudlarking or coastal fossil-hunting. Neap tides are the least extreme, with the smallest movement, and they fall in between the spring tides.

Spring tides: 5th–7th and 20th–22nd

Neap tides: 13th–15th and 27th–29th

Spring tides are shaded in black in the chart opposite.

August tide timetable for Dover

For guidance on how to convert this for your local area, see page 8.

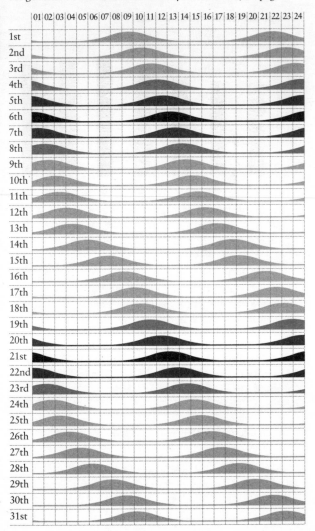

THE SKY

Stars, meteor showers and planets

We have one of the better meteor showers coinciding with a dark sky this month, so there is a chance of some good trails. Mars and Jupiter will stay close together for the middle part of the month, which is worth looking out for, with Mars rather dimmer than Jupiter. Saturn will get higher and brighter as it approaches opposition next month. It will rise in the evening, reaching its height in the early hours, and on the 21st it will be occulted by the moon – it will slip behind it for almost an hour.

12th–13th: Perseid meteor shower. Best time for viewing is from 22.00 to 03.00. A low half moon sets by 23.30, leaving a dark sky.
14th: Close approach of Jupiter and Mars. They will rise at 00.40 in the northeast and reach an cerem of 40 degrees in the east before becoming lost in the dawn at around 05.00.
20th–21st: Close approach of Saturn and the nearly full moon, and occultation of Saturn. They will rise at about 21.20 in the east and reach an altitude of 30 degrees in the south by 02.00. At around 04.25 Saturn will be occulted by the moon, which means that it will disappear behind it. The exact time depends on location, so it would be sensible to start looking at least 30 minutes before this. Binoculars on a steady mount give a clearer view. Saturn will reappear approximately 50 minutes later but will probably be lost in the dawn.
27th: Close approach of Mars, Jupiter and the moon. They will rise just before midnight in the northeast and reach 50 degrees altitude in the east before becoming lost in the dawn at around 05.30.

The sun

20th: At solar noon (approximately 13.00 BST/IST) the sun will reach an altitude of 50 degrees in the London sky and 46 degrees in the Glasgow sky.

Sunrise and set

Coton in the Elms, Derbyshire

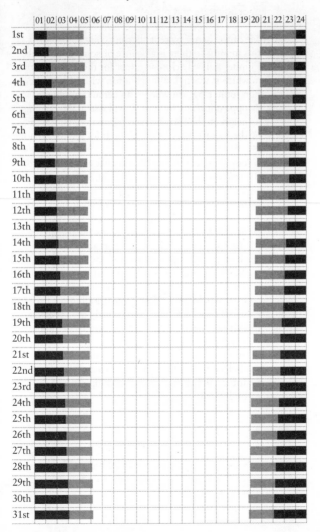

Moonrise and set

Like the sun, the moon rises roughly in the east and sets roughly in the west. It rises about 50 minutes later each day. Use the following guide to work out approximate moonrise times.

Full moon: Rises at around sunset time, but opposite the sun, so in the east as the sun sets in the west.
Last quarter: Rises at around midnight, and is at its highest point as the sun rises.
New moon: Rises at sunrise, in the same part of the sky as the sun, and so cannot be seen.
First quarter: Rises at around noon, and is at its highest point as the sun sets.

Moon phases

New moon – 4th August, 12.13	
First quarter – 12th August, 16.18	
Full moon – 19th August, 19.25	
Last quarter – 26th August, 10.25	

The times given above are for the exact moment each moon phase occurs, for instance the moment that the moon is at its fullest.

August's full moon is known as the Grain Moon or Lynx Moon.

Moon phases for August

1st	2nd	3rd	4th NEW	5th
6th	7th	8th	9th	10th
11th	12th	13th	14th	15th
16th	17th	18th	19th FULL	20th
21st	22nd	23rd	24th	25th
26th	27th	28th	29th	30th
31st				

MEDITATIONS

August's influences and guidance from Louise Press

August arrives with a collective 'out breath'. There is a sigh in the air, brought about by the summer holidays, feelings of having achieved and looking ahead to harvest. It feels like a very welcome pause: permission to rest and relax as the nation takes its foot off the pedal. However, towards the end of the month we feel a change as we prepare to gear up for the cogs to start whirring again into a new season.

On 1st August, Lammas is celebrated. This is the first of three harvest festivals marked by baking bread using grain from the first gathering-in from the fields. In Ireland on the 1st, Lughnasadh, the third of the Celtic fire festivals, is a feast for the Sun God, Lugh, and thanksgiving for our earth as mother. We can begin to examine our own harvest. Are the fruits of our labour beginning to ripen?

The new moon in Leo rises on 4th August, offering us the opportunity to check in with ourselves. Where are we feeling strong? Can we identify our vulnerabilities? The dark night of the new moon is when our inner truth reveals itself. Leo is heart-centred, with a strong inner fire. Although outwardly confident, this astrological sign encourages us to show up as we are – no hiding behind the mask of who others think we should be. This new moon is all about finding the courage to be ourselves, speak our truth, let the sun in and radiate our warmth.

Interestingly, the full moon on 19th August reaches her peak in the change-making sign of Aquarius. The theme of the last couple of weeks will continue as Aquarius illuminates us as individuals and shines a light on how we operate out in the world as a force for good. Towards the end of this month, we will be encouraged to question, challenge and push boundaries. This full moon invites us to be curious about our conditioning. Who influences us? What stories shape us? What is our piece in the universal jigsaw? It's time to find our voice in the crowd and use it for the greater good of all.

Making a space for August

Now that we are into the first of the harvest months, you might want to look to the harvest table as an inspiration for the space in which you mark the month. See what berries are starting to come to maturity in the hedgerows – or even just pick a few rose hips from the park. Arrange some of them on your table, perhaps alongside your proudest vegetable garden achievements on their way to the kitchen. Colours now are turning towards the autumnal, whether we like it or not, so reflect that in your space.

Your table this month might include:
- A golden-yellow tablecloth and candles
- A vase of sunflowers
- A vase of grass seed heads
- An ear of corn
- A bundle of wheat stems
- A loaf of bread, for Lammas
- A bowl of blackberries

Light your candles for Lammas, and think about the harvest that you have gathered on your table, the bounty of the months to come, and everything that has gone into making it come about.

A

GARDENS

Gardening by the moon

The following is a guide to gardening with the phases of the moon, according to traditional practices. For moon-gardening cynics it also works as a guide to the month's gardening if you disregard the exact dates.

Last quarter to new moon: 28th July–4th August (until 12.13) and 26th August–2nd September

A dormant period, with low sap and poor growth. Do not sow or plant. A good time though for pruning, while sap is slowed. Weeding now will check growth well. Harvest any crops for storage. Fertilise the soil. Garden maintenance.

- Deadhead dahlias to keep new flowers coming.
- Weed regularly.
- Continue to feed tomatoes regularly with a high potash feed, and tie the stems in as they grow. Once a plant has produced 4–5 trusses (6–7 on some cherry types), 'stop' the plant by nipping out the tip, which encourages ripening.
- Pinch out the tips of climbing beans when they reach the tops of their frames.
- Earth up potatoes.
- Tie in the new growth of blackberries and boysenberries so their stems are horizontal or even slope downwards.

New moon to first quarter: 4th (from 12.13)–12th August (until 16.18)

The waxing of the moon is associated with rising vitality and upward growth. Towards the end of this phase, plant and sow anything that develops crops above ground. Prepare for growth.

- Also towards the end of this phase you can sow, plant out or take cuttings of all of those things mentioned in the first quarter to full moon phase.

First quarter to full moon: 12th (from 16.18)–19th August

This is the best time for sowing crops that develop above ground, but is bad for root crops. Pot up or plant out seedlings and young plants. Take cuttings and make grafts but avoid all other pruning. Fertilise.

- Sow hardy annual flowers where you want them to bloom next year.
- Sow salad leaves for autumn and winter harvesting: mustard greens, mizuna, mibuna, pak choi and chop suey greens, as well as kale, rocket, lettuce and Swiss chard.
- Take cuttings of scented geraniums to overwinter.
- Feed everything.

Full moon to last quarter: 20th–25th August

A 'drawing down' energy. This phase is a good time for sowing and planting any crops that develop below ground: root crops, bulbs and perennials.

- Sow your last batch of carrots and turnips.
- Plant strawberry plants.
- Sow green manures to protect bare soil over winter: alfalfa, field beans, grazing rye or phacelia.

Note: Where no specific time for the change between phases is mentioned, this is because it happens outside of usual gardening hours. For exact changeover times for any late-night or pre-dawn gardening, refer to the August moon phase chart on page 176.

A

GARDEN CRAFT

Flower and leaf mandalas

A part of Buddhist and Hindu traditions, mandalas involve making beautiful concentric patterns, often with coloured sand. They act as a focal point for a moment of calm, and you can use the flowers and leaves in the late summer garden to make one of your own. Choose a still day and make your mandala on the ground, or take flowers and leaves indoors.

You will need:
    Flowers and leaves

Choose one flower for the centre of your mandala. Break open your larger flowers so that you have lots of individual petals to work with. You could put them straight onto the ground or lay large leaves down first, placing them in a circle, on which to position the flowers. Keep on working, adding more rings of flowers and leaves, until you have created a beautiful, colourful and textured piece of temporary nature art.

A

NATURE

Garden wildlife in August

As the season progresses, bumblebee queens start producing new queens and males, as well as workers. These leave the nest to mate with bees from other nests. The males die soon after mating but the queens continue to feed ahead of hibernation, storing the males' sperm until they need it the following spring.

There is a switch in the diet of garden birds this month, which often goes unnoticed as most birds are lying low and moulting (losing and growing new feathers). Those that have fed on earthworms, grubs and insects throughout the year now feast on berries, in preparation for migration. Berries are rich in calories and antioxidants, which help relieve the physical stresses of long flights to warmer climes.

Hoglets, now boasting new spikes and vision, will join their mother on foraging trips, where she will teach them to find food and what to eat. She will continue to feed them milk in the nest as well. Towards the end of the month, the hoglets will start to explore alone. Once fully independent, they will live solitary lives and will remain solitary, apart from when seeking a mate.

It's a sad time in the sky, as by the middle of the month it has emptied of swifts. They don't waste any time after chicks have fledged, and set off on the journey back south as soon as they are able. You may spot swallows gathering on telephone wires, they will remain for another month, while house martins – which sometimes have a third brood – can stay into October.

Soil teems with life at this time of year, as earthworms and other invertebrates, including springtails and woodlice, digest spent plant material such as leaf litter. This is turned into smaller particles that are then consumed by bacteria, fungi and even viruses, or soil microbes, which 'recycle' nutrients back to plant roots. Together, these make up the soil fauna that keeps the wonderful world beneath our feet ticking over. Soils high in organic matter, or spent plant material, have the most soil fauna. The highest concentrations of fauna are around plant roots themselves, the area known as the rhizosphere.

THE KITCHEN

Cooking from the garden in August

Here are some crops that you might find in the kitchen garden this month: sweetcorn, tomatoes, aubergines, French beans, runner beans, calabrese, fennel, courgettes, leeks, radishes, globe artichokes, beetroot, cabbages, carrots, cauliflowers, chard, cucumbers, endive, garlic, lettuces, shallots, onions, spring onions, sweet peppers, chilli peppers, peas, potatoes, wild rocket, spinach, turnips, marjoram, thyme, dill, basil, mint, oregano, plums, apples, pears, blackcurrants, blueberries, loganberries, melons, raspberries, redcurrants, strawberries, cherries.

Ideas for eating from the garden this month

- *Pan con tomate*, consisting of your biggest and ripest tomato grated over a bowl, a piece of toast with garlic rubbed in and then topped with the grated tomato, olive oil and salt.
- Raw runner beans cut on the diagonal and dipped into bagna cauda – a hot sauce of olive oil, anchovies and garlic.
- Quick pickled cucumber ribbons with poached salmon and dill yogurt.
- Sweetcorn barbecued and topped with butter, salt, lime juice and chilli flakes.
- Raspberries simmered, strained and simmered again until syrupy, then poured over vanilla ice cream or over ice cream and peaches in a pretty glass bowl for peach melba.

A

SNACK OF THE MONTH

Okonomiyaki (savoury Japanese pancakes)

Obon, the Japanese Buddhist festival of the dead, falls on 15th August. It is traditional to gather with family to remember ancestors, and to light lanterns outside of houses and set them adrift on lakes and rivers, to guide the ancestors back home. There are also carnivals with rides, dances and street food. *Okonomiyaki* is a Japanese pancake and a street food served at these occasions, particularly in Osaka, from where it originates. *Okonomi* means 'as you like it' and *yaki* means 'grilled'. It comprises chopped cabbage and various other fillings of your choice cooked in a dashi-flavoured batter, then topped with a special *okonomiyaki* sauce and toppings. Make large pancakes and cut them into segments or smaller ones, as shown here.

Makes about 6 medium pancakes

150g plain flour

1 teaspoon baking powder

2 eggs, lightly beaten

20g panko breadcrumbs

200ml dashi (or use water)

1 tablespoon salt

1 teaspoon sugar

2 teaspoons white wine vinegar

1 large garlic clove, finely grated

2 mushrooms, finely diced

100g Savoy cabbage, thinly sliced

50g protein of your choice, such as cubed tofu, cooked chopped prawns or cooked pork (optional)

rapeseed oil, for frying

For the *okonomiyaki* sauce and toppings

3 tablespoons tomato ketchup

2 tablespoons oyster sauce

2 tablespoons Worcestershire sauce

Japanese Kewpie mayonnaise or ordinary mayonnaise in a squeezy bottle, to taste

1 sheet nori seaweed, thinly sliced

2 spring onions, thinly sliced

20g sushi ginger, thinly sliced

pinch of bonito flakes (optional)

Method

For the *okonomiyaki* sauce, mix together the ketchup, oyster sauce and Worcestershire sauce.

For the batter, put the flour, baking powder, eggs, panko breadcrumbs, dashi or water, salt, sugar and vinegar in a bowl and whisk together until smooth. Stir in the garlic, mushrooms, cabbage and protein, if using.

Heat a little oil in a frying pan over a medium heat. Place two heaped tablespoons of the mixture into the frying pan, pushing it out a little to make a thick round. Fry for around 4 minutes, or until golden brown, then flip it over. Smear the top liberally with *okonomiyaki* sauce and cook for around another 4 minutes, or until the bottom is golden brown. Repeat with the rest of the mixture.

Once cooked, transfer the pancakes to serving plates and draw thin zigzags of mayonnaise all over the surface. Top with the seaweed, spring onions, ginger and bonito flakes, if using, and serve immediately.

FOLK SONG

'Garden Hymn'
Traditional, arr. Richard Barnard

'Garden Hymn' is an old American hymn, and is in the Sacred Harp choral-singing tradition, which originated in New England and was perpetuated in the American South. Sacred Harp songs are always sung unaccompanied, with four singers each taking a turn in leading. 'Garden Hymn' is thought to have found its way to the British Isles via a visiting preacher around 1804.

The Lord into His garden come,
The spices yield their rich perfumes,
The spices yield their rich perfumes,
The lilies grow and thrive;
Refreshing showers of grace divine
From Jesus flow to every vine,
From Jesus flow to every vine,
Which make the dead revive.

O, that this dry and barren ground
In springs of water may abound,
In springs of water may abound,
A fruitful soil become;
The desert blossoms as the rose,
While Jesus conquers all His foes,
While Jesus conquers all His foes
And makes His people one.

A

GARDEN SPECIAL

Autumn nectar-rich plants

Many wild flowers have packed up shop now, so this is a crucial time for the gardener to step in and provide nectar-rich flowers for the bees and pollinating insects. A good source at this time of year can make a huge difference to the success of insects like bumblebees, currently getting ready to overwinter.

It is now the best planting time of the year, for perennials and for bulbs, so look back through this year's nectar-rich plant lists and see what you can plant now for next year's insects.

Michaelmas daisy, *Aster amellus*: One of several daisy flowers that bring pollen to the autumn garden. The flowers are small and produced en masse, generally in shades of purple or pink, and are mobbed by bees on sunny autumn days.
Purple coneflower, *Echinacea purpurea*: Purple petals surround an orange centre, which is made up of a great many tiny flowers, each containing its own well of nectar.
Black-eyed Susan, *Rudbeckia hirta*: Another autumn daisy-like flower, this time with striking bright yellow petals surrounding a black centre.
Stonecrop, *Hylotelephium spectabile (syn. Sedum spectabile)*: These produce flat heads of many tiny pink flowers, providing a perch for insects to sit and drink up their nectar.
Japanese anemone, *Anemone hupehensis* and *Anemone × hybrida*: While the other plants on this autumn list would happily grow side by side in a border, Japanese anemone is a bit of a thug and needs space of its own. It produces pink flowers on long, elegant stems. 'Honorine Jobert' is a pure white variety.

BLACK-EYED SUSAN

JAPANESE ANEMONE

PURPLE CONEFLOWER

MICHAELMAS DAISY

STONECROP

September

1 Start of meteorological autumn

7 Ganesh Chaturthi – birth of Ganesh (Hindu)

8 Paralympics 2024 Closing Ceremony, Stade de France, Paris

11 Enkutatash – Ethiopian New Year (Rastafarian)

15 Prophet Muhammad's birthday (Islamic) begins at sighting of the crescent moon

22 Autumn equinox, at 13.43 – start of astronomical autumn

22 Mabon – harvest celebration (Pagan)

29 Michaelmas Day (Christian/traditional)

SEPTEMBER IN THE GARDEN

Onion skins turn papery and their shoots grow yellow, which announces...harvest time. In the still-muggy greenhouse, aubergines are black and shiny, and dripping clusters of tomatoes grow heavy with juice, the glass misting up against the cooling air beyond. Apples lie on the wet lawn, turning the air cidery in the low golden sun. The gardener selects three, carefully turning them for wasps, stretches a hand wide to hold them, and thinks ahead to the cooling evening, and the first apple crumble of the year.

Rains have swelled the garden, and perked up the late flowers. Clouds of purple Michaelmas daisies and ghostly Japanese anemones fill the borders, along with their flame-coloured daisy friends, rudbeckia and sunflowers, bees bumbling among them gratefully: the last nectar stop. Vibrant crocosmia arches between transparent flowering heads of ornamental grasses, and dahlias are in their prime: glowing, saturated colours in the newly gentle September light.

There's a hint of a chill in the equinox air as the hemisphere turns away from the sun. The Harvest Moon rises over the garden, fat and yellow. In response the gardener fills the kitchen with an unlikely alliance of the excess and the unripe – green tomatoes and marrows, plums, onions and pears tumbling onto the kitchen table. The fug of vinegar, spices and sugar drifts up through the house as this harvest is thrown together and put away. Tops are screwed onto hot jars, little white labels marked 'Sept. '24' are pressed onto rounded glass. Dark cupboards are filled neatly with jarfuls of the summer garden to mellow and eventually accompany the Christmas ham.

An ancient sigh, a calling home, into the dark half of the year. Something is complete, but here there is a new beginning. The gardener crouches, digs holes, drops bulbs into them, nestles them into the chilling earth, then tucks away the promise of spring. It will sit beneath the earth all winter long, to emerge the next time day and night are equal.

Garden and weather folklore

Check your onion skins as you harvest them to tell if the coming winter is going to be harsh:

> *'Onion skin thin, a mild winter coming in,*
> *Onion skin thick and tough, coming winter cold and*
> *rough.'*

There is some thought that this folklore could be linked to La Niña years. This weather phenomenon – the cold counterpart to warm El Niño – is characterised by a dry summer or even a summer drought, which would lead to thickened skins on onions, followed by a cold winter.

Michaelmas Day on 29th September is traditionally the end of the harvest season, and is another one of the saints' days that set the tone for the weather of the following period: 'As the wind is on St Michael's Day, so it will be for three months.'

Clear weather on Michaelmas Day is also a sign of a long, cold winter in Irish folklore: 'Michaelmas Day be bright and clear there will be two "winters" in the year.'

A widespread belief in 'equinoctial gales' – an increase in winds around the time of the equinox – is sadly not backed up by evidence. However, the sun's waning hold on the northern hemisphere's weather systems around this time can allow for bad weather to roll in from the north Atlantic, and the autumn equinox can often be a moment when the weather turns more autumnal, and so windier, just as you would expect.

S

THE SEA

Average sea temperature in Celcius

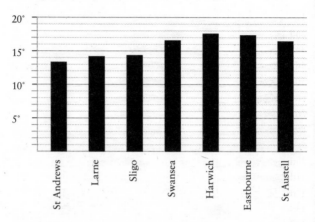

Spring and neap tides

Spring tides are the most extreme tides of the month, with the highest rises and the lowest falls, and they follow a couple of days after the full moon and new moon. These are the times to choose a low tide and go rock-pooling, mudlarking or coastal fossil-hunting. Neap tides are the least extreme, with the smallest movement, and they fall in between the spring tides.

Spring tides: 4th–6th and 19th–21st

Neap tides: 12th–14th and 25th–27th

Spring tides are shaded in black in the chart opposite.

September tide timetable for Dover

For guidance on how to convert this for your local area, see page 8.

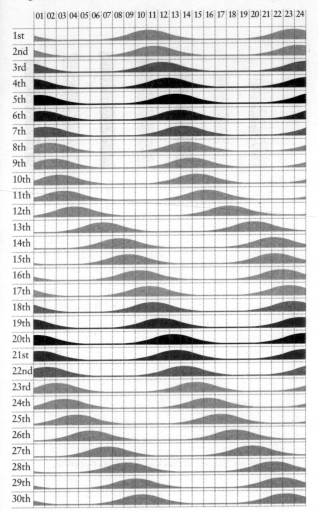

THE SKY

Stars, meteor showers and planets

Saturn will be at opposition this month, at its highest and brightest, rising around 20.00 in the east and visible all night until setting in the west at dawn. Mars and Jupiter will rise in the northeast around midnight and be high in the sky by dawn.

5th: Mercury's greatest elongation west, when it is furthest from the sun and easiest to see. It will be visible for a few days either side of this date. In the morning, look towards the direction of sunrise, close to the horizon, shortly before the sky starts to get light at around 04.30. Not an easy planet to spot.
8th: Saturn at opposition. It will rise around 20.00 in the east and reach its maximum height of 30 degrees around midnight in the south before setting in the west around 06.00.
23rd–24th: Close approach of the moon and Jupiter. They will rise in the northeast overnight and become lost at dawn.
25th: Close approach of Mars and the moon, rising just before midnight in the northeast then lost in the dawn at around 06.20.

The sun

22nd: Autumn equinox. The autumn equinox falls at 13.43, the moment when the centre of the sun is directly above the equator. It will occur again at the spring equinox in March.
22nd: At solar noon (approximately 13.00 BST/IST) the sun will reach an altitude of 38 degrees in the London sky and 34 degrees in the Glasgow sky.
25th: Equilux. It is commonly believed that day and night are of equal length on the equinox. This is not quite the case, as we measure day length using the moment the top of the sun appears over or disappears below the horizon, rather than the moment the centre of the sun is on the horizon. Equilux is when day and night are actually the same length and it occurs around 25th September this year in the UK and Ireland.

Sunrise and set

Coton in the Elms, Derbyshire

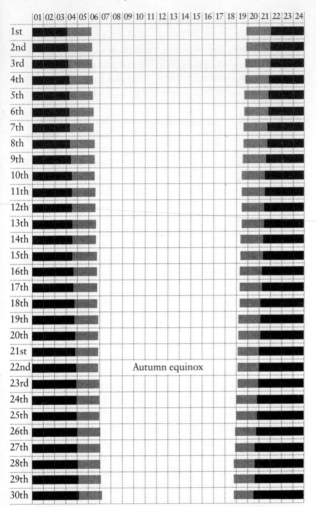

Autumn equinox

Moonrise and set

Like the sun, the moon rises roughly in the east and sets roughly in the west. This month also sees a Supermoon, but please refer to page 176 for details of how to work out approximate moonrise times.

Moon phases

New moon – 3rd September, 02.55

First quarter – 11th September, 07.05

Full moon – 18th September, 03.34

Last quarter – 24th September, 19.49

The times given above are for the exact moment each moon phase occurs.

When September's full moon is the closest full moon to the autumn equinox, as occurs this year, it is known as the Harvest Moon. It can also be known as the Wine Moon or Song Moon.

This is the first of three super full moons, or supermoons, this year. A supermoon is also known as a perigee-syzygy of the earth-moon-sun system – the moon's imperfect orbit brings it to one of its closest points to the earth at the same moment as the moon is full. A supermoon occurs when the centre of the moon is less than 360,000 kilometres from the centre of the earth. It can appear up to 14 per cent bigger and 30 per cent brighter than when the full moon is at its furthest point in the cycle.

This full moon will also be subject to a partial lunar eclipse, but there will not be much to see as the moon barely touches the earth's shadow. There may be a slight dimming of the moon's edge at around 03.40 on the 18th as it passes through the earth's penumbra, the area of the earth's shadow outside of the core or 'umbral' shadow.

Moon phases for September

1st	2nd	3rd NEW	4th	5th
6th	7th	8th	9th	10th
11th	12th	13th	14th	15th
16th	17th	18th FULL	19th	20th
21st	22nd	23rd	24th	25th
26th	27th	28th	29th	30th

S

MEDITATIONS

September's influences and guidance from Louise Press

As September arrives we begin to relinquish our outer energy and adjust our focus inwards once again. Guided by the season, we can take time this month to reflect on our own inner harvest. All around us, berries, apples, hips and nuts have ripened. This is a time of gratitude for the abundance of life; for gathering in and sharing with friends, family, community and beyond. The autumn equinox on the 22nd, marking the moment of balance between light and dark, is the moment in the year when we cross from our outer expression to our inner reflection.

We kick off with a new moon in Virgo on the 3rd, which calls us home to ourselves after the expansion of the last few months. Summer is filled with outer action and expenditure of energy, which is wonderful for the soul but can permeate our energetic boundaries. Virgo reminds us to shore up our self-protection once again and prepare to focus on our inner health and wellbeing. It's time to sort the wheat from the chaff. We can ask ourselves questions such as: What plans have been fruitful and what actions have not served us so well? By doing this we fill our autumn basket with goodness and let go of the rest.

We are treated to a super full moon and partial lunar eclipse on the 18th in the sign of Pisces. A super full moon, or supermoon, being closer and therefore appearing larger and brighter than usual, has a greater energetic influence on life on earth, emphasising our intentions and strengthening our actions. By its nature, a full moon reveals. What will this emotionally sensitive Pisces energy reveal in us this month? We may feel our vulnerabilities as we begin to shed our outer layers and prepare for autumn. We may also pick up on subtle energies around us: the mood of our loved ones, our community and the wider web of society. It's important not to dismiss what we pick up; Pisces is the ancient mystic and she lives in us all.

Making a space for September

This month we celebrate the Harvest Moon and the equinox, and so the nature table is likely to reflect the bounty of this moment. Gather from hedgerows and the garden and make up bowls of produce interspersed with the first falling leaves. If you can find a brown cloth to use, it will enhance the deepening golden colours of the display.

Your table this month might include:
- Yellow, orange and red candles
- Autumn leaves
- A bowl of your home-grown tomatoes, aubergines and peppers
- A corn dolly
- A bowl of acorns and nuts
- A jam jar of late summer flowers
- A pomegranate

Light your candles at the moment of the equinox, at 13.43 on 22nd September. Think about what this moment means, stepping into the darker half of the year, and of all the joys that it brings: the candles and the fires, the warm jumpers and the cosy evenings indoors, the striding out into the bracing cold, and the retreating back indoors.

S

GARDENS

Gardening by the moon

The following is a guide to gardening with the phases of the moon, according to traditional practices. For moon-gardening cynics it also works as a guide to the month's gardening if you disregard the exact dates.

Last quarter to new moon: 26th August–2nd September and 25th September–2nd October

A dormant period, with low sap and poor growth. Do not sow or plant. A good time though for pruning, while sap is slowed. Weeding now will check growth well. Harvest any crops for storage. Mulch the soil. Garden maintenance.

- Lift maincrop potatoes and prepare them for storage.
- Pick apples and pears for storage. Wrap them individually in paper and place in crates.
- Once a tomato plant has produced 4–5 trusses (6–7 on some cherry types), you need to 'stop' the plant by nipping out the tip, to encourage ripening rather than further growing.
- Deadhead dahlias to prolong flowering.
- Order spring bulbs.
- Stop feeding house plants and reduce watering towards the end of the month.
- Bring tender plants inside towards the end of the month.
- Save seed from favourite flowers or crops.

New moon to first quarter: 3rd–10th September

The waxing of the moon is associated with rising vitality and upward growth. Towards the end of this phase, plant and sow anything that develops crops above ground. Prepare for growth.

- Also towards the end of this phase, sow, plant out or take cuttings of all of those things mentioned in the first quarter to full moon phase.

First quarter to full moon: 11th–17th September

This is the best time for sowing crops that develop above ground, but is bad for root crops. Pot up or plant out seedlings and young plants. Take cuttings and make grafts but avoid all other pruning.

- Sow hardy annual flowers where you want them to bloom next year.
- Sow salad leaves and cover with cloches: mustard greens, mizuna, mibuna, pak choi and chop suey greens, as well as kale, rocket, lettuce and Swiss chard.
- Sow sweet peas in the greenhouse or cold frame for early flowers next year.
- Compost summer bedding once it has gone over, and seek out winter bedding – foliage, pansies, violas and heathers – to plant up in pots and hanging baskets.
- Plant out wallflowers for a spring display.
- Take cuttings of scented geraniums to overwinter indoors on a windowsill.

Full moon to last quarter: 18th – 24th September

A 'drawing down' energy. This phase is a good time for sowing and planting any crops that develop below ground: root crops, bulbs and perennials.

- Plant autumn bulbs. Daffodil bulbs in particular need to go in by the end of this month.
- Plant up forced hyacinth bulbs and paperwhites from late September to early October so they will have a chance of being in flower for Christmas.
- Plant onion sets.
- Plant new perennials in your flower borders, and lift, divide and replant those that have finished flowering.

Note: Where no specific time for the change between phases is mentioned, this is because it happens outside of usual gardening hours. For exact changeover times for any late-night or pre-dawn gardening, refer to the September moon phase chart on page 200.

GARDEN CRAFT

Making leaf skeletons

Leaves are starting to turn and soon will be falling. Very
occasionally you will find leaf skeletons in the garden: those
that have been subject to the exact conditions that allow for the
fleshy parts to rot away, and for microorganisms to move in and
remove the remnants, but dry and sheltered enough for the
skeleton to remain intact. You can recreate these conditions,
and create your own leaf skeletons to make into autumnal
garlands, turn into cards, or just have as delicate ornaments.

You will need:
    1 litre water
    1 tablespoon bicarbonate of soda
    1 tablespoon baking powder
    Saucepan
    Leaves
    Soft-bristled toothbrush
    Kitchen paper

Put the water, bicarbonate of soda and baking powder into the
saucepan and bring to the boil. Drop in the leaves. Simmer for
about an hour – topping up with more water if it starts to boil
dry – and then remove a leaf to test. The pulp should brush
away leaving the skeleton behind. If it doesn't, return it to the
pot for another 15 minutes and try again.

    In a shallow tray of cold water, brush the pulp off with
the toothbrush. Leave the skeleton to dry on a piece of
kitchen paper.

S

NATURE

Garden wildlife in September

As we head into autumn, an old bumblebee queen will lay fewer and fewer eggs, and eventually she and her nest will come to a natural end. Meanwhile, her mated daughters will be feeding on the last of the year's nectar in readiness for hibernation.

Some bees are only just emerging from hibernation, however. The ivy bee is the latest bee on the wing in the UK, flying in the month of September. As their name suggests, these solitary bees feed mostly on ivy flowers, and they nest – often in huge aggregations – in sandy soils, including lawns.

Garden birds are establishing autumn territories this month, with this year's young competing with older birds that are returning to their patch after the summer moult. While most of this takes place fairly amicably, robins and wrens can defend their territories fiercely, and you may spot the odd skirmish.

Some hedgehogs will mate for a second time this month, particularly in the milder south. Food starts to become scarce in autumn, so this can be a huge gamble that doesn't always pay off, as babies emerging from nests in October are rarely able to gain enough weight to see them through hibernation.

As annual plants set seed and die, and perennials and trees shed leaves and store sugar in their roots, there is less available food for soil microbes, which slow down and settle into a quiescent state. Meanwhile, fungal networks start sending up fruiting bodies – mushrooms – this month, which provide food for a range of species like field mice and beetles, while helping create the next generation of fungi. Most mushrooms exist for just a short time, releasing spores into the wind, before dying back into the soil. These spores survive in a dormant state in winter, ready to inoculate new ground and send out new hyphae when temperatures increase again.

THE KITCHEN

Cooking from the garden in September

Here are some crops that you might find in the kitchen
garden this month: tomatoes, aubergines, chillies, sweet
peppers, runner beans, French beans, peas, beetroot,
calabrese, cabbages, carrots, cauliflowers, chard, courgettes,
cucumbers, endive, fennel, garlic, kale, leeks, lettuces, onions,
spring onions, shallots, swedes, sweetcorn, Oriental leaves,
pumpkins, winter squashes, wild rocket, spinach, turnips,
basil, mint, dill, oregano, thyme, marjoram, apples, pears,
loganberries, autumn raspberries, blackberries, plums,
redcurrants, figs, grapes.

Ideas for eating from the garden this month
- A purple and white salad of radicchio, smashed
  blackcurrants, goats' cheese and toasted hazelnuts.
- Focaccia topped with red grapes and fennel seeds.
- Very ripe beefsteak tomato drizzled with olive oil,
  sprinkled with salt and left to marinate, eaten later with
  torn basil, burrata and bread to mop up the juices.
- Fig and thyme upside-down cake.
- Apple and sultana crumble with lots of cinnamon in the
  fruit, served with vanilla ice cream.

S

SNACK OF THE MONTH

Berenjenas fritas (fried aubergine) with truffle honey

If there looks to be a glut of aubergines, then now is the time to make these little sweet-and-salty fried aubergine sticks to nibble on. Aubergines and truffle are beautiful together, and the spices are subtle but faintly autumnal too.

Serves 2
1 large aubergine
2 tablespoons salt
50g plain flour
1 teaspoon ground cinnamon
1 teaspoon smoked paprika
6 tablespoons rapeseed oil
a handful of flat leaf parsley, chopped
½ tablespoon truffle honey, to drizzle

Method

Cut the aubergine in half across the middle. Stand each half on its cut end and slice through it 4 times evenly in both directions, to create long batons. Place them in a sieve over a bowl and toss in the salt. The salt will flavour the flesh and draw out the moisture, which will help the finished dish crisp up. Leave them to stand for 1 hour, rinse to remove the salt and dry thoroughly with a clean tea towel or kitchen paper.

Mix the flour, cinnamon and paprika together and toss the aubergine pieces in the mixture to coat thoroughly. Heat the oil in a deep frying pan until hot. Add the aubergine batons in small batches so as not to overcrowd the pan. Fry for 2–3 minutes, moving them around to ensure even colouring. Once crisp and golden, lift them onto a plate lined with kitchen paper to drain. Repeat with the rest of the aubergine.

Once cooked and cooled slightly, scatter over the parsley, drizzle with truffle honey and enjoy while warm and crisp.

Baked apples with Campari

One of the simplest ways to enjoy cooking apples is to remove the core, fill it with something sweet and autumnal, and then bake the whole thing until it slumps and the flavours meld together. This is gorgeous without the alcohol, but the Campari lends notes of citrus and herb, and the hint of bitterness (and booze) does make the whole thing feel more adult. You might also try it with a shot of rum instead.

Serves 2

50ml Campari

2 large Bramley apples, cored

30g sultanas

30g ground almonds

2 tablespoons rolled oats

½ teaspoon almond extract

50g light brown sugar

50g butter, cubed

vanilla ice cream and runny honey, to serve (optional)

Method

Use a small baking dish that the apples will fit snuggly into. Pour the Campari into the dish and place the apples on top. Combine the sultanas, ground almonds, rolled oats, almond extract and half the sugar in a bowl then pack the mixture into the centres of the apples. Scatter the cubed butter and remaining sugar over the top of the apples. Cover with a piece of dampened and scrunched up baking parchment or with kitchen foil, tucking it around the apples so that they steam. Preheat the oven to 190°C, Gas Mark 5 and cook the apples for 35 minutes. Remove the parchment or foil and return to the oven for 5–10 minutes, for a bit of caramelising action on top. Allow to cool a little before eating the apples with the juices poured over and with a drizzle of honey and a scoop of vanilla ice cream, if liked.

S

FOLK SONG

'The Sprig of Thyme'
Traditional, arr. Richard Barnard

This song, a warning to young women about feckless lovers, plays heavily with the Victorian idea of the language of flowers. There are two possible meanings to the titular 'thyme'. It can just be a play on words, 'let no man steal your thyme/time', but it is also thought to represent virginity, and the rue in the song is associated with bitterness and regret. The song finds us in a garden past its prime and overrun with weeds, looking back at its glory days of summer.

    'The Sprig of Thyme' is closely associated with 'The Seeds of Love', our song for June, and often the lyrics and tunes are cross-pollinated. The two are sometimes thought of as variations of the same song from different perspectives. This melody is a version sung by Mrs Jarret in Somerset in 1908.

Come all you pretty fair maids
That are all in your prime,
I would have you weed your garden so clear
And let no man steal your thyme.

For once I had a sprig of thyme,
It prospered by night and day
Till a false young man came a-courting to me
And he stole my thyme away.

O, thyme it is a precious thing,
That grows all under the sun
And thyme will bring all things to an end
And so does my thyme grow on.

But now my garden's overrun
And in it no flowers grew,
For the beds that once had the sweetest of thyme
They are now overrun with rue.

Now it's very well drinking ale
And it's all well drinking wine,
But it's far better sitting by a young man's side
That has gained this heart of mine.

S

October

1   Harvest Home/Ingathering (traditional)

1   Start of Black History Month

2   Rosh Hashanah/Jewish New Year, start of the Jewish year 5785, begins at sundown

10   Old Michaelmas Day (Christian/traditional)

11   Yom Kippur, Day of Atonement (Jewish), begins at sundown

16   Sukkot/First day of Feast of Tabernacles (Jewish) begins at sundown

21   Apple Day

27   British Summer Time and Irish Standard Time end. Clocks go back one hour at 02.00

28   October bank holiday, Ireland

31   Halloween

OCTOBER IN THE GARDEN

Morning mists lie across the gardens, accompanied by mellowing leaves and the scent of softening earth. Everything is giving up, triggered by the light, which fades and shortens daily. Autumn is settling, and pulling the garden down into itself. Leaves cut off by the cold from their supply of green-giving chlorophyll begin to flash their reds, yellows and golds, before they tumble.

There is faint wood smoke on the cool air, and a treasure hunt is on. The gardener's fork is pushed in, the earth is levered up and the hidden harvest reveals itself among the startled and squirming worms. Potatoes are laid out on the ground like a catch, to cure. The gardener thinks of chips, fried and scented with vinegar, or mash made creamy with full fat milk and topped with a pool of butter. Pumpkins and squashes also lie in the autumn sun of crisp blue-sky days, and their deeply burnished orange, green, yellow and blue-grey skins, echoing the leaves, harden to preserve the marigold insides deep into winter. There is the crinkled blue-black of cavolo nero still standing proud, and apples by the basketful, wrapped in newspaper and then placed in crates for a rainy day, of which there will be many.

In the flower border the time of seeds is here. Flowers are transforming into their skeletons – firework allium heads, sea holly spikes, sedum heads like rolling hills – holding up their offerings to age with the winter frosts and rains, slowly give up, break apart and scatter. They fall to cold earth, and wait until it warms again, so many months from now, to then form a small family of seedlings around their mother's skirts. Berries want just the same, but they hope to do it via the birds that will pluck them whole and carry them away, depositing them to start their new lives in the richest possible growing medium. They gleam with health and colour, saying 'eat me'.

There are still some flowers, the outliers. Chief of all is the beautiful funeral flower the chrysanthemum, with its rust or yellow petals, soft white or acid green – forever shunned for blooming at this time of death and decay.

Garden and weather folklore

If there is a period of warm weather towards the end of October, it is called St Luke's Little Summer. It is said to start around St Luke's Day, on the 18th, and be brought to an abrupt close by St Simon and St Jude, who share the 28th as their feast day. Simon and Jude also pop up as summer busters in a rhyme about Michaelmas daisies, which are always in flower on Michaelmas Day, 29th September.

> 'The Michaelmas Daisies, among dead weeds, bloom for
>   St Michael's valorous deeds.
> And seems the last of flowers that stood, till the feast of
>   St Simon and St Jude.'

However the two saints don't always bring things to a halt, as there is also the possibility of All Hallows Summer, unseasonably warm weather around All Hallows Eve (Halloween) which is on the 31st. In Greece there is the Little Summer of St Demetrios, which sometimes spans the last two weeks of the month and is a final burst of good weather, allowing sheep to be led to winter grazing fields.

Old Michaelmas Day falls on 10th October (or some say 11th October), a result of the calendar reform of 1752 when 11 days were lost. This is the day on which Michael threw the Devil out of heaven. He landed on a blackberry bush and cursed it or spit on it or worse. It is not a good idea to pick and eat blackberries after this date.

O

THE SEA

Average sea temperature in Celcius

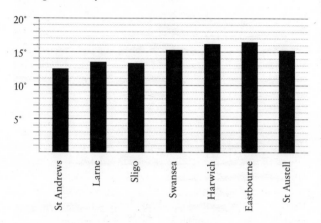

Spring and neap tides

Spring tides are the most extreme tides of the month, with the highest rises and the lowest falls, and they follow a couple of days after the full moon and new moon. These are the times to choose a low tide and go rock-pooling, mudlarking or coastal fossil-hunting. Neap tides are the least extreme, with the smallest movement, and they fall in between the spring tides.

Spring tides: 3rd–5th and 18th–20th

Neap tides: 11th–13th and 25th–27th

Spring tides are shaded in black in the chart opposite.

October tide timetable for Dover

For guidance on how to convert this for your local area, see page 8.

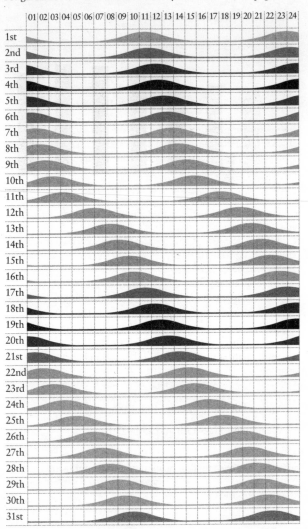

THE SKY

Stars, meteor showers and planets

By mid-month Jupiter will rise at 21.00 in the northeast. It will be high in the sky in the south by 04.00 before getting lost in the dawn around 07.00. Mars will follow the same path as Jupiter, but rising some two hours later. Saturn will become visible in the dusk in the southeast and will set in the west.

14th: Close approach of Saturn and the moon. They will first appear in the dusk at around 18.40 in the east at an altitude of 13 degrees. They will reach a maximum height of 30 degrees in the south at 22.30 and will set in the west at around 03.20 the next day.
20th–21st: Close approach of the moon and Jupiter. They will rise around 20.50 in the northeast and become lost in the dawn at around 07.00 the next day.
23rd: Mars, the moon, Jupiter and Saturn are all visible. Look around 01.00 from northeast to southwest.
23rd–24th: Close approach of Mars and the moon. They will rise around 23.00 in the northeast and reach 60 degrees altitude in the south before becoming lost in the dawn at around 07.00.

The sun

2nd: Annular eclipse of the sun. An annular eclipse is when the moon covers the centre of the sun, leaving a 'ring of fire' around the edge. It will be visible from the eastern Pacific Ocean and the southern tip of South America to the South Sandwich Islands but unfortunately not from the UK and Ireland.
21st: At solar noon (approximately 13.00 BST/IST) the sun will reach an altitude of 28 degrees in the London sky and 24 degrees in the Glasgow sky.

Sunrise and set
Coton in the Elms, Derbyshire

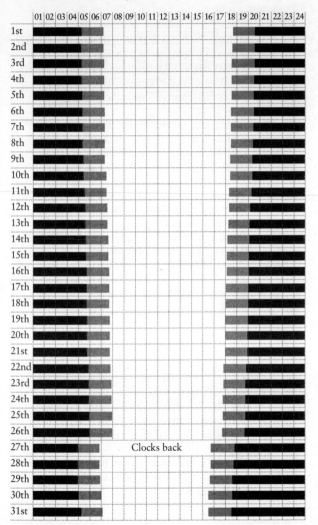

British Summer Time and Irish Standard Time end on 27th October at 02.00 and this has been accounted for above.

Moonrise and set

Like the sun, the moon rises roughly in the east and sets roughly in the west. It rises about 50 minutes later each day. Use the following guide to work out approximate moonrise times.

Full moon: Rises at around sunset time, but opposite the sun, so in the east as the sun sets in the west.
Last quarter: Rises at around midnight, and is at its highest point as the sun rises.
New moon: Rises at sunrise, in the same part of the sky as the sun, and so cannot be seen.
First quarter: Rises at around noon, and is at its highest point as the sun sets.

Moon phases

New moon – 2nd October, 19.49	●
First quarter – 10th October, 19.55	◐
Full moon – 17th October, 12.26	○
Last quarter – 24th October, 09.03	◑

The times given above are for the exact moment each moon phase occurs, for instance the moment that the moon is at its fullest.

October's full moon is known as the Hunter's Moon or Blood Moon. It is the second of three super full moons, or supermoons, this year (see page 200).

Moon phases for October

1st	2nd NEW	3rd	4th	5th
6th	7th	8th	9th	10th
11th	12th	13th	14th	15th
16th	17th FULL	18th	19th	20th
21st	22nd	23rd	24th	25th
26th	27th	28th	29th	30th
31st				

O

MEDITATIONS

October's influences and guidance from Louise Press

Our first autumn new moon opens this month with an annular solar eclipse on the 2nd. Although not visible from the northern hemisphere, it is present through its transformational energy.

Our new moon rises in the orderly sign of Libra and its focus is relational. As we begin our descent into the darker months, now is a good time to invest in our relationships. Our number one relationship is with ourselves. Where can we improve on a little self-love? Once we've filled our own cup, we are in a good position to assess where we're giving ourselves away too liberally or perhaps not giving enough. Are we living a life of reciprocity from a place of fullness? We witness this giving for the greater good in the natural world around us. The earth surrenders her summer allure at this time to feed the winter decay process. This in turn will nourish roots ready for new life in the spring. There is so much we can learn from being a conscious part of this reciprocal partnership and cycle of life.

The 17th brings the second supermoon of the year (see page 200). This time in the fire sign of Aries. Ruled by Mars and motivated by action, this supermoon has the potential to reveal aspects of our personality we like to keep hidden…our shadow selves. Aries advocates for its own needs well, which can sometimes lead to a lack of consideration for others. It is possible to achieve our own goals without trampling on others to get there. The motivational energies present at this time gift us with the opportunity to make personal change. Let's be mindful of the lessons we learned under the new moon and take care of our relationships.

On 31st October–1st November is the fourth, and last, Celtic fire festival of the year: Samhain, or Halloween as most people recognise it nowadays. Traditionally this time was important to celebrate the final harvest of the year and mark our descent into winter. It's a time to honour ancestors and others who have gone before us, for without them there would be no harvest to celebrate.

Making a space for October

You might be hard-pressed to make an October table that doesn't reflect upcoming Halloween, so why not lean into it? Combine your nature finds with spiders' webs and skeletons, and a bowl of nuts or acorns that can be emptied and filled with sweets on the 31st.

Your table this month might include:

- Orange and black candles and cloths
- A bowl of acorns or nuts
- Apples
- Pumpkins – carved or otherwise
- Skulls
- Autumn leaves
- Bare twigs
- A bowl of sweets for Halloween

As nights and mornings are dark now, you can light your candles often to create a cosy glow among your autumnal table finds. Make sure to light them on Halloween if you are expecting little ghoulish visitors to come knocking.

The fire festival of Samhain, Halloween's precursor, straddles the end of October and the beginning of November. If you are not a fan of Halloween, look ahead to Making a space for November (page 247) for an alternative approach.

O

GARDENS

Gardening by the moon

The following is a guide to gardening with the phases of the moon, according to traditional practices. For moon-gardening cynics it also works as a guide to the month's gardening if you disregard the exact dates.

Last quarter to new moon: 25th September–2nd October and 24th October–1st November (until 12.47)

A dormant period, with low sap and poor growth. Do not sow or plant. A good time though for pruning, while sap is slowed. Weeding now will check growth well. Harvest any crops for storage. Garden maintenance.

- Lift maincrop potatoes and prepare them for storage.
- Lift and store beetroot. Turnips will need to come up before the ground freezes. Carrots and parsnips can stay in the ground until needed, and parsnips will be improved by a little frost.
- Cut pumpkins and winter squashes on a fine day and leave to 'cure' in the sun, then store them somewhere frost-free.
- Pick apples and pears for storage.
- Cover salad leaves and leafy vegetables with cloches to keep them in good condition through winter.
- Dismantle supports for runner beans, peas and tomatoes.
- Pick green tomatoes and make chutney or put them into paper bags and store in a dark place where they can ripen slowly.
- Earth up Brussels sprouts and other brassicas to prevent them from rocking in the wind, and earth up leeks to blanch the stems.

New moon to first quarter: 3rd–10th October

The waxing of the moon is associated with rising vitality and upward growth. Towards the end of this phase, plant and sow anything that develops crops above ground. Prepare for growth.

- Towards the end of this phase you can sow, plant out or take cuttings of all of those things mentioned in the first quarter to full moon phase.

First quarter to full moon: 11th–17th October (until 12.26)

This is the best time for sowing crops that develop above ground, but is bad for root crops. Pot up or plant out seedlings and young plants. Take cuttings and make grafts but avoid all other pruning.

- Sow broad beans for early summer crops next year, either direct into the ground or in pots in the greenhouse.
- Sow hardy varieties of pea in place and cover them with cloches, or sow in pots or guttering in a greenhouse. Do the same for sweet peas.
- Plant out spring-flowering wallflowers, violas and forget-me-nots.

Full moon to last quarter: 17th (from 12.26)–23rd October

A 'drawing down' energy. This phase is a good time for sowing and planting any crops that develop below ground: root crops, bulbs and perennials.

- Plant up hyacinth, paperwhite and hippeastrum bulbs in early October to have a chance of flowers for Christmas.
- Plant spring bulbs and corms – last chance for daffodils, perfect timing for crocuses, scilla, fritillaries and irises.
- Plant lilies and ornamental alliums.
- Plant garlic cloves and overwintering onion sets.
- Plant rhubarb crowns and bare root fruit bushes.
- Plant new grapevines, peaches and nectarines.
- Plant new herbaceous perennials in your flower borders. Lift, divide and replant those that have finished flowering.

Note: Where no specific time for the change between phases is mentioned, this is because it happens outside of usual gardening hours. For exact changeover times for any late-night or pre-dawn gardening, refer to the October moon phase (see page 222).

GARDEN CRAFT

Make Halloween nature wands

Two methods are included here for making a Halloween nature wand. The first produces a beautiful 'jewelled' wand, while the second is a quick and easy wand a child can make while simultaneously enjoying a nature walk or a Halloween party.

For a 'jewelled' wand, you will need:
>   A stick about 30cm long
>   Coloured threads, such as wool or embroidery
>   thread offcuts
>   Feathers, leaves, seed heads and beads

Tie a thread around one end of the stick and use it to secure a special feather or pair of colourful leaves, then continue winding it around the stick to create a band of colour. Work down the stick in this way, using different coloured threads and different found objects, interspersed with beads.

For a make-as-you-go wand, you will need:
>   A stick about 30cm long
>   Double-sided sticky tape or masking tape
>   Tray of autumnal nature finds (optional)

Wind double-sided sticky tape around the stick, or do the same with masking tape with the sticky side facing outwards. The child can now take their wand on a nature walk and collect items by sticking them to the wand as they go. Or for a Halloween party activity, give children a tray of objects that you have gathered yourself.

O

229

NATURE

Garden wildlife in October

Most bumblebee nests have finished now, with daughter queens tucked – alone – into wax-lined holes in the soil, in compost heaps, leaf piles and even plant pots, waiting out winter until they can establish a new nest in spring and start laying eggs.

While many species are disappearing for winter, some are arriving. Redwings and fieldfares turn up from Scandinavia this month, along with waxwings and smaller birds like hawfinches and bramblings. They usually feed on berries and seeds in the countryside but will visit gardens if sources of natural food run dry. Leaving windfall apples where they land can be perfect for winter migrants, while growing seeding and berrying plants will provide more food for years to come.

On sunny days butterflies may still be on the wing, feasting from the last of the summer flowers. Some, such as the peacock and small tortoiseshell, hibernate as adults, taking shelter beneath shed roofs or in outhouses. Traditionally a summer migrant, the red admiral should fly south for winter, but many stay in the UK thanks to our milder winters, and may emerge on sunny days to feed. Others hibernate as caterpillars, pupae or eggs, and are far less conspicuous.

As the temperatures drop, adult hedgehogs continue to eat as much as possible to gain weight, and begin building their nests ready for hibernation. They hibernate in similar situations to where the females raise their young – under a hedge, in a compost heap or in leaf pile.

October is a month of abundance, and colourful jays, along with squirrels, will start caching nuts now. Both species are fond of acorns and will bury them in the ground, to save for later. They don't always get around to eating their stores of winter food, however, and, you may find little oak trees popping up in all sorts of places around the garden, come spring.

THE KITCHEN

Cooking from the garden in October

Here are some crops that you might find in the kitchen garden this month: aubergines, chillies, sweet peppers, green tomatoes, beetroot, Brussels sprouts, cabbages, carrots, cauliflowers, celeriac, celery, chard, chicory, endive, fennel, garlic, kale, leeks, lettuces, onions, Oriental leaves, parsnips, potatoes, salsify, scorzonera, spinach, spring onions, swedes, turnips, winter squashes, chervil, parsley, coriander, sage, rosemary, bay, medlars, quince, apples, pears, grapes.

Ideas for eating from the garden this month
- Crescent moons of roasted winter squash and slices of grilled halloumi, dressed with balsamic vinegar, toasted walnuts and parsley.
- Pak choi stir-fried and tossed with garlic, ginger, fish sauce and lime juice, with noodles and steamed fish.
- Irish stew – beef chuck, carrots, celery and potatoes slow-cooked in stout and stock.
- Cinnamon sugar sprinkled on buttered toast, then topped with apple slices fried in butter.
- Quince poached in wine with star anise until deep pink, served with brown sugar meringues and clotted cream.

O

SNACK OF THE MONTH

Stamp and Go (salt cod fritters) for Black History Month

Stamp and Go are salt cod fritters originating in Jamaica. There are a couple of potential explanations for the name: some say that it originates on British naval ships, where the order to do something quickly was 'stamp and go', while others say it originates with the many street food vendors who make it, because of customers stamping their feet impatiently for their delicious cod fritters. Traditional salt cod can be found in Spanish and Jamaican food shops and in some larger supermarkets. It has a specific and quite meaty texture. If using it, you will need to soak it for at least 48 hours (check the instructions) before you plan to cook. You can also use fresh cod for this recipe, and 'quick salt' it, see the instructions opposite.

Makes 20 fritters

160g skinless cod (fresh or salt)

175g plain flour

½ teaspoon bicarbonate of soda

1 onion, sliced and fried in a little oil until soft and translucent

1 teaspoon chilli flakes

1 teaspoon dried oregano

½ teaspoon ground allspice

2 spring onions, sliced

1 large tomato, finely diced

20g curly parsley, finely chopped

grated zest of 1 lemon

1 teaspoon salt

½ teaspoon ground black pepper

100ml rapeseed oil, for deep frying

Method

If using salt cod, soak it according to the instructions on the packet, changing the water every 8 hours or so. Taste a little piece to check it is not still too salty; if it is, leave it to soak for longer. Drain it, put it in a heatproof bowl and pour boiling water over it. Drain it again just before you start to cook, and fork the fish into flakes.

If using fresh cod, use the 'quick salt' method: cut the cod into pieces of even thickness and place them on a dish covered in salt, then cover the tops with salt (you'll need about the same weight of salt as cod). Leave to firm up in the refrigerator for a few hours. Rinse off the salt.

Preheat the oven to 180°C, Gas Mark 4. Place the fish in an ovenproof dish with a little olive oil, scrunch up some baking parchment to soften it and use it to cover the fish. Bake for 15–20 minutes, or until the flesh is opaque. Fork into flakes.

To make the fritters, put the flour and bicarbonate of soda in a bowl and whisk in 120ml water to make a batter. Stir in the rest of the ingredients, including the fish, except the oil. The mixture shouldn't be too wet; you might need to add a little more flour. Fill a pan or deep-fryer one third full with oil and heat it to 180°C, or until a cube of bread dropped into it turns golden brown in 15 seconds. Carefully add spoonfuls of the fritter mix, being careful not to overcrowd the pan. Fry each one for a few minutes on each side, then lift onto a plate lined with kitchen paper and eat as soon as they are cool enough to do so. Serve with your favourite hot sauce.

O

FOLK SONG

'Rosemary Lane'

Traditional, arr. Richard Barnard

Another song, like September's 'The Sprig of Thyme', that
uses the fading of the garden as an analogy for a life ruined
by seduction. Here the maid is convinced by her sailor lover
that any child that arises from their union will be well taken
care of, but it is clear from the final verse that it all came
to nothing.

I was once in ser-vice down Rose-ma-ry__ Lane; I kept the good
will of my__ mas-ter and dame, then__ one fate-ful day a young
sail-or came by and this was the__ start of my mi - se - ry.

I was once in service down Rosemary Lane;
I kept the good will of my master and dame,
Then one fateful day a young sailor came by
And this was the start of my misery.

The sailor was drowsy, he hung down his head,
He asked for a candle to light him to bed.
I led him there too, as another might do,
He said, 'Pretty maid, won't you come to bed too?'

Next morning so early the sailor arose
And into my apron three guineas he throws,
'Take every last one, for I have done so wrong,
I've left you a daughter or else a fine son.

'And if it's a girl she shall sit at her ease,
And if it's a boy he shall sail the salt seas,
With jacket so blue and his ribbons and bows
He'll climb the high rigging where e're the wind blows.'

Now all you young lasses take warnings from me
Beware the young sailor whoe'er he may be.
Like a flower in the garden when its beauty's all gone
You will be left with nothing, with naught to be done.

O

November

1 Samhain – celebration of the beginning of winter, cross-quarter day (Gaelic/Pagan)

1 All Saints' Day (Christian)

1 Diwali – festival of lights (Hindu/Sikh/Jain)

2 All Souls' Day (Christian)

2 Bridgwater Guy Fawkes Carnival and procession

5 Guy Fawkes Night

10 Remembrance Sunday

11 Remembrance Day

11 Martinmas (Christian/traditional)

21 Beaujolais Nouveau Day

24 Stir-up Sunday

28 Thanksgiving (US traditional)

30 St Andrew's Day, patron saint of Scotland – bank holiday, Scotland

NOVEMBER IN THE GARDEN

Apples turned in glossy toffee. A bonfire crackling against a starry sky, flames leaping to the trees. Shouts and gasps across the gardens as chrysanthemum fireworks light everything starkly and momentarily in pink and white. And in the hours that follow, the bonfire's slow dying down to glowing embers, cups of still-warm spiced cider keeping the stragglers warm.

The next morning a web snaps across the gardener's face, the spiders having reclaimed the garden overnight. A spent rocket languishes on the lawn, and the misty morning air is still scented by the bonfire embers. Under the hedge and among the shrubs, mushrooms erupt in soft whites, greys and browns – sulphur tuft, liberty cap, shaggy ink cap, fairy ring mushroom. The year might be winding down for most of nature, but this is the height of it for the mushrooms. All year their networks of mycelium have worked their way through the earth, and now is their moment to lift their heads, spread their gills and release their delicate spores into the damp air. The microscopic potential life forms alight on the wind, then settle onto the moist earth and prepare to spread their own networks deep and wide.

The gardener pulls up their collar, and plants the tulip bulbs under the earth. They are the last bulbs of the year to be sunk down, a Samhain offering to the darkness, shoring up the return of the light, and of pinks, purples, yellows and reds. The garden is turning monotone, and as colour drains, structure and texture step forward in the form of rough bark, skeleton seed heads and arching grass stems that wave in the breeze.

The gardener lifts the rake and sweeps green arcs. Gold, brown and orange leaves are gathered into wet, papery piles, until the changing wind teases the leaves, undoes them and sends the gardener back indoors for a mug of tea. The garden will be left alone often now, viewed occasionally from the back window, the panes steaming up.

Garden and weather folklore

Samhain on the 1st November was long considered the
beginning of winter, after a great feast thrown on the 31st
October to say a final farewell to any remnants of summer.
Just as at the beginning of the year, there are a couple of
pieces of weather lore that suggest that whatever the weather
is now, it will not last:

> 'Ice in November to bear a duck,
> Nothing after but mud and muck.'

> 'On the first of November if weather hold clear,
> An end to what sowing you do to this year.'

Despite the cold and dark there is still the possibility of an
Indian summer, a term that is often used for any spell of mild
and sunny autumnal weather but which specifically means
a warm spell on the nine days between Martinmas, on the
11th November, and the 20th November. It is characterised by
sunny, hazy days and is also known as Martinmas summer.

Martinmas is said to hold particular sway in setting the
direction of the wind, and therefore the severity of the rest
of winter. 'If the wind is southeast on Martinmas, it will stay
there till Candlemas' and so will make for a mild winter. On
the other hand, if it is a north wind, this suggests a hard
winter to come.

St Catherine's Day, the 25th, was the day to look
further ahead:

> 'At St Catherine's, foul or fair,
> So it will be next Februair.'

And finally, St Andrew's Day, on the 30th November, was
known in Sweden as Andersdagen or Anders and was
traditionally used to forecast the weather for Christmas Day.
Anders slaskar, julen braskar, means 'slushy St Andrew's Day,
frozen Christmas'.

N

THE SEA

Average sea temperature in Celcius

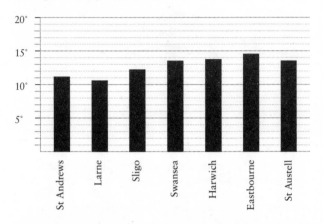

Spring and neap tides

Spring tides are the most extreme tides of the month, with the highest rises and the lowest falls, and they follow a couple of days after the full moon and new moon. These are the times to choose a low tide and go rock-pooling, mudlarking or coastal fossil-hunting. Neap tides are the least extreme, with the smallest movement, and they fall in between the spring tides.

Spring tides: 2nd–4th and 16th–17th
Neap tides: 9th–11th and 24th–26th

Spring tides are shaded in black in the chart opposite.

November tide timetable for Dover

For guidance on how to convert this for your local area, see page 8.

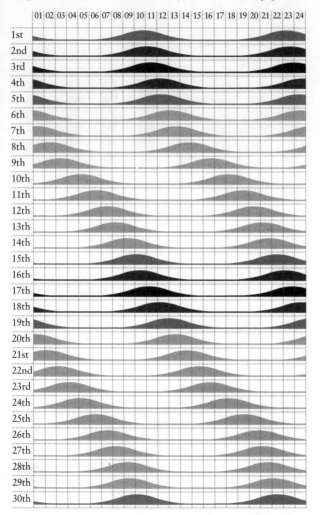

THE SKY

Stars, meteor showers and planets

By mid-November, Jupiter will rise after dusk in the northeast. It will be high in the southern sky by midnight and then go on to be lost in the dawn. Mars will have brightened and be easy to spot. It will follow the same path as Jupiter after rising in mid-evening. Saturn will rise at around dusk in the southeast. It will reach an altitude of 30 degrees by 19.00 in the south and will set around midnight in the west. Having hidden from us for most of the year, Venus will make a brief appearance each day at around 16.30 in the southwest before setting at 18.00.

10th: Close approach of Saturn and the moon. They will first appear in the dusk at around 17.00 in the southeast at an altitude of 20 degrees. They will set in the southwest around midnight.

17th–18th: Close approach of the moon and Jupiter. They will rise at around 17.40 in the northeast and become lost in the dawn at about 06.30 the next day.

20th–21st: Close approach of Mars and the moon. They will rise at around 20.40 in the northeast and reach 50 degrees altitude in the southwest before becoming lost in the dawn by 06.50 the next day.

The sun

21st: At solar noon the sun will reach an altitude of 18 degrees in the London sky and 14 degrees in the Glasgow sky.

Sunrise and set

Coton in the Elms, Derbyshire

	01	02	03	04	05	06	07	08	09	10	11	12	13	14	15	16	17	18	19	20	21	22	23	24
1st																								
2nd																								
3rd																								
4th																								
5th																								
6th																								
7th																								
8th																								
9th																								
10th																								
11th																								
12th																								
13th																								
14th																								
15th																								
16th																								
17th																								
18th																								
19th																								
20th																								
21st																								
22nd																								
23rd																								
24th																								
25th																								
26th																								
27th																								
28th																								
29th																								
30th																								

N

Moonrise and set

Like the sun, the moon rises roughly in the east and sets roughly in the west. It rises about 50 minutes later each day. Use the following guide to work out approximate moonrise times.

Full moon: Rises at around sunset time, but opposite the sun, so in the east as the sun sets in the west.
Last quarter: Rises at around midnight, and is at its highest point as the sun rises.
New moon: Rises at sunrise, in the same part of the sky as the sun, and so cannot be seen.
First quarter: Rises at around noon, and is at its highest point as the sun sets.

Moon phases

New moon – 1st November, 12.47	⬤
First quarter – 9th November, 05.55	◑
Full moon – 15th November, 21.29	◯
Last quarter – 23rd November, 01.28	◐

The times given above are for the exact moment each moon phase occurs, for instance the moment that the moon is at its fullest.

November's full moon is known as the Darkest Depths Moon or Mourning Moon.

This month's full moon is the last of this year's super full moons, or supermoons (see page 200).

Moon phases for November

1st NEW	2nd	3rd	4th	5th
6th	7th	8th	9th	10th
11th	12th	13th	14th	15th FULL
16th	17th	18th	19th	20th
21st	22nd	23rd	24th	25th
26th	27th	28th	29th	30th

N

MEDITATIONS

November's influences and guidance from Louise Press

November's mantra is 'Let go and release'. Do as the world around you is doing; boldly step into a place of surrender. It's not a pushing away, there is no effort in it…be like the trees that drop their leaves, and just let go of anything that no longer serves you. We don't want to take anything into the nurturing darkness of winter that will take root unconsciously. We want to pick out our metaphorical weeds before they spread, ready to pop up again into our lives next spring.

The moon's energies are beautifully counterbalanced this month, at the doorway of winter. There is work to do as we cross the threshold into the darkest months of the year with a lightness of heart. November kicks off with a sting in its tail. A new moon rises on the 1st in Scorpio. Scorpio can be a harsh yet deeply healing and insightful teacher should you feel courageous enough to heed its lessons. Aligned with the seasonal energies of release, this new moon challenges us to look beneath at the things we bury about ourselves – the things we cover up and don't want others to see. Scorpio requires us to unpack it all, take a good look, deal with it one way or another and move on unencumbered. It's time to free ourselves from any emotional baggage that's holding us back.

The full moon in Taurus arrives on the 15th to gather up any unresolved issues that require closure following our new moon interrogations this month. Scrutinising Scorpio energies at the beginning of the month make way for the deeply grounding and steadying presence of Taurus. This full moon can help us complete and integrate lessons learned this year, dissolve any residual blockages and steady ourselves ready for the nourishing, intuitive dream time of winter. Aligned with the world around us, hibernation is the order of the season, and under this earthy Taurus full moon we will be called to nest. Security, home, comfort and nourishing food are the guiding principles of late November. It's time to get cosy.

Making a space for November

The cusp of October and November brings with it many traditions that serve as invitations to mourn and to remember those that we have lost, and this can provide a beautiful way of using a November nature table, echoing European All Souls' Day traditions on the 1st and Mexico's *Día de Muertos* (Day of the Dead) on the 2nd. Samhain, which straddles October and November, is thought to have been a festival to mark the beginning of winter and to honour ancestors. Fill your table with photographs of your own ancestors, mementos of them and scraps of poetry. Surround them with chrysanthemums, the flowers traditionally used in France to decorate graves on All Souls' Day, and with your seasonal finds.

Your table this month might include:

- Autumn leaves
- A bowl of chestnuts
- Chrysanthemums in oranges, yellows and reds
- Orange or white candles
- Pictures of loved ones who have died
- Bare twigs
- Mushrooms
- Pumpkins
- Apples

Light your candles and think about those that you have lost, maybe taking a moment to write down a few thoughts that you can tuck into the nature table. Think too about the countryside at the moment, how everything is closing down and dying, but that light and life and spring will come around again.

N

GARDENS

Gardening by the moon

The following is a guide to gardening with the phases of the moon, according to traditional practices. For moon-gardening cynics it also works as a guide to the month's gardening if you disregard the exact dates.

Last quarter to new moon: 24th October–1st November (until 12.47) and 23rd–30th November

A dormant period, with low sap and poor growth. Do not sow or plant. A good time though for pruning, while sap is slowed. Weeding now will check growth well. Harvest any crops for storage. Mulch the soil. Garden maintenance.

- Prune apple, pear, medlar and quince trees.
- Prune grapevines before the winter solstice.
- Remove the nets from fruit cages. Prune gooseberries and red and white currants.
- Remove any figs that haven't ripened.
- Check your soil's pH level and add lime or calcified seaweed to raise the pH if below 6.5, and make nutrients more easily available.
- Mulch beds with organic manure.
- Pick apples and pears for storage.
- Lift dahlias after they have been blackened by the first frost. Dry them out and store the tubers in moist sand somewhere cool but frost-free.
- Weed thoroughly. This is a good time to get ahead with any perennial weed problems.
- Prune roses.
- Collect up fallen leaves and stuff them into leaf mould bins or into bin bags with a few holes punctured.

New moon to first quarter: 1st (from 12.47)–8th November

The waxing of the moon is associated with rising vitality and upward growth. Towards the end of this phase, plant and sow anything that develops crops above ground. Prepare for growth.

- Towards the end of this phase, you can sow, plant out or take cuttings of all of those things mentioned in the first quarter to full moon phase.

First quarter to full moon: 9th–15th November

This is the best time for sowing crops that develop above ground, but is bad for root crops. Take cuttings and make grafts but avoid all other pruning.

- Sow broad beans for early summer crops next year, either direct into the ground or in pots in the greenhouse.
- Sow hardy varieties of pea in place and cover them with cloches, or sow in pots or guttering in a greenhouse. Do the same for sweet peas.

Full moon to last quarter: 16th–22nd November

A 'drawing down' energy. This phase is a good time for sowing and planting any crops that develop below ground: root crops, bulbs and perennials.

- Plant tulips. Plant summer-flowering lily and ornamental allium bulbs.
- Plant paperwhite, miniature iris and forced hyacinth bulbs for late-winter indoor flowers.
- Plant garlic cloves and overwintering onion sets.
- Plant rhubarb crowns and bare root fruit bushes, new grapevines, peaches, nectarines, apples, pears, quince and medlar.
- Plant new peaches and nectarines.
- Plant new flowering perennials. Lift, divide and replant those that have finished flowering.

Note: Where no specific time for the change between phases is mentioned, this is because it happens outside of usual gardening hours. For exact changeover times for any late-night or pre-dawn gardening, refer to the November moon phase chart on page 244.

N

GARDEN CRAFT

Preserving leaves

Beautiful autumn leaves gradually fade and lose their colour over time. This is a way to preserve them, then you can string them together into garlands, create falling-leaf mobiles, or use them to make pictures or cards. There are two methods of preserving: one for single leaves and the other for whole stems.

For single leaves you will need:
    Colourful single leaves
    Shallow tray or vase
    Glycerine (from pharmacies and many supermarkets)
    Pebbles
    Kitchen paper

Place the leaves in the shallow container and make up a mixture of one part glycerine to two parts water – just enough to cover the leaves. Use pebbles to weigh down the leaves. Leave to soak for five days, then remove and pat dry with kitchen paper.

For a whole stem/branch you will need:
    A stem or branch of autumn leaves
    Bucket of warm water
    Glycerine
    Vase
    Hammer

First immerse the stem into a bucket of warm water for about two hours. Mix up a solution of one part glycerine to two parts water in a vase, filling it to at least halfway. Recut the stem and then use the hammer to bash the base of the stem until it is mashed and broken apart, to allow for greater absorption of the glycerine. Place the branch in the vase out of direct sunlight. Beads of glycerine solution will appear on the tips of the leaves when they have soaked up all they can, after about five days. Remove from the solution and hang it upside down to dry.

NATURE

Garden wildlife in November

On sunny and mild days it can appear as though autumn hasn't arrived yet. Dragonflies and butterflies may still be on the wing, while the last of the year's hoverflies and wasps will be feasting on the dregs of the ivy flowers. Yet all of these species will have hibernacula (shelters in which to overwinter) to go to and, as temperatures drop, they will disappear.

In their pre-made hibernacula, lined with dry leaves and moss, hedgehogs settle down and their body temperature drops to match their surroundings, so they enter a state of torpor. They need to weigh around 600g to have enough fat reserves to survive hibernation. Those that don't – including last month's 'autumn orphans' – will continue feeding throughout winter. This can be a dangerous time as food is in short supply, so you can help by leaving out cat biscuits for them. And if you see a hedgehog out during the day, call your local rescue centre for advice, as it will almost certainly need taking in.

While most species are tucked up and asleep, garden birds are awake, seeing out the few hours of daylight each day. This is a difficult time for birds, as low temperatures and short days mean they need more food but have less time to find it. When it's cold, birds fluff up their feathers to trap heat, as well as shivering to keep warm. With their high metabolic rate, they can burn a lot of calories doing this. They scour branch tips, buds and the skeletal remains of plants to seek out overwintering insects, and they turn leaves on the ground to search for morsels sheltering beneath them. Seeds, berries and rose hips are important sources of winter food, and we can help by not cutting back plants or tidying away leaves in our gardens. Filling feeders with seeds and suet balls can also help to give them the calories they need, although natural food is always best. And we must keep feeders clean to prevent the spread of diseases like avian pox and trichomonosis.

THE KITCHEN

Cooking from the garden in November

Here are some crops that you might find in the kitchen
garden this month: cabbages, cardoons, carrots, celeriac,
celery, chard, chicory, endive, kale, leeks, lettuces, onions,
spring onions, shallots, Oriental leaves, parsnips, potatoes,
pumpkins, winter squashes, salsify, scorzonera, spinach,
swedes, turnips, chervil, parsley, coriander, sage, rosemary,
bay, quinces, medlars, pears.

Ideas for eating from the garden this month
- Carrots roasted in honey and za'atar arranged on a bed of
  creamy hummus, sprinkled with chopped parsley.
- Potato, swede and celeriac boulangère, all sliced thinly
  and layered together with onions, thyme and stock, then
  slow-cooked until tender and the top is browned.
- Onion and rosemary tarte tatin, served with a herby sauce
  or parsley pesto.
- Spiced winter squash soup, finished off with lots of lime
  juice and topped with crème fraîche, bacon bits and fried
  sage leaves.
- Chocolate and pear cake, made with rye flour.

N

SNACK OF THE MONTH

Roast chestnuts with honey and cumin

Roast chestnuts, split and eaten with butter and salt, are an excellent winter snack, and this is just a slightly fancier version, perfect for eating huddled around the fire on Bonfire Night. Here, pre-peeled chestnuts are used, but of course you can also use chestnuts you have harvested and laboured out of their skins yourself. They are also good stirred through buttery greens or Brussels sprouts, or chopped and sprinkled over ice cream.

Serves 2–4

1 packet (180g) cooked whole chestnuts

2 tablespoons sesame seeds

1 tablespoon olive oil

1 tablespoon sesame oil

1 tablespoon runny honey

1 teaspoon salt

1 teaspoon cumin seeds, toasted and crushed in a pestle and mortar

½ teaspoon cayenne pepper (optional)

Method
Preheat the oven to 200°C, Gas Mark 6. Using a clean tea towel or kitchen paper, pat the chestnuts dry. Cut the big ones in half. Put them in a bowl with all the other ingredients and mix well, making sure the nuts are well covered. Spread them out on a baking tray and roast for about 20 minutes, checking halfway through and giving them a stir to make sure they are toasting evenly. Allow to cool a little before eating.

Pumpkin *barfi*

Diwali is the Hindu, Sikh and Jain festival of lights. Candles are lit and traditional sweets, such as *barfi*, are prepared and shared with friends and neighbours. This version is made with in-season pumpkin, but you could also try winter squash.

Makes about 20 pieces
200g pumpkin, peeled and cut into 1cm cubes
175ml milk
200g chickpea flour
175g caster sugar
100g ghee, plus more for greasing
1 heaped tablespoon ground cardamom
½ teaspoon rose water
2 tablespoons black sesame seeds

Method

Preheat the oven to 190°C, Gas Mark 5. Place the pumpkin in a roasting dish with a splash of water and tuck a large, damp and scrunched up sheet of baking parchment over it. Cook for 30 minutes. Allow to cool, then blitz with the milk, using a blender or a stick blender, to a smooth paste.

Sieve the chickpea flour into a large frying pan over a medium heat and move it around with a spatula for a few minutes until it browns and releases a nutty aroma – be careful, the flour can catch and burn quickly. Add the sugar and the milky pumpkin mix. Reduce the heat and use a hand whisk for a minute or two to combine into a thick, smooth paste. Gradually add the ghee and whisk to combine until the mixture pulls cleanly away from the side of the pan. Turn off the heat, add the cardamom and rose water and combine.

Grease a shallow tray with ghee and pour in the mixture, pressing firmly and evenly into a 1cm-thick layer. Sprinkle over the sesame seeds and press down to secure. Score with a knife into pieces. After an hour or so in a cool place, it will be set and ready to lift out of the tin and cut into pieces.

N

FOLK SONG

'The Life of a Man'
Traditional, arr. Richard Barnard

This folk song uses the cycle of a tree through the seasons as a metaphor for the life of a man, with autumn and the first frosts now upon us and the leaves withering and falling. An alternative name for this widespread folk song is 'The Fall of the Leaf'.

As I was out walking one morning at ease,
A-viewing the leaves as they hung on the trees,
They all were in motion, appearing to be,
And those that were withered, they fell from the tree.
What's the life of a man any more than the leaves?
A man has his season, so why should he grieve?
Although in this world he appears bright and gay,
Like a leaf he shall wither and soon fade away.

I saw those same leaves but a short time ago,
They all were in motion, appearing to grow,
When frosts came upon them and withered them all,
Then the rain it did follow and down they did fall.
What's the life of a man any more than the leaves?
A man has his season, so why should he grieve?
Although in this world he appears bright and gay,
Like a leaf he shall wither and soon fade away.

If you go to the church many names you will see,
Who fell from this world like the leaves from the trees.
Old age and affliction all on us will call,
Like the leaves we will wither and down we shall fall.
What's the life of a man any more than the leaves?
A man has his season, so why should he grieve?
Although in this world he appears bright and gay,
Like a leaf he shall wither and soon fade away.

N

GARDEN SPECIAL

Winter nectar-rich plants

There are very few insects around now, but on mild days overwintering insects can venture out, and if their bravery is rewarded with a stomach full of nectar, they will be more likely to make it through the many cold days to come.

Common ivy, *Hedera helix*: Wonderful for flowering just as most flowers are closing down for winter, and you will often find flowering ivy buzzing with bees topping up on nectar before the cold weather sets in.
Evergreen clematis, *Clematis cirrhosa*: A beautiful and delicate climber that flowers in winter and will provide the odd passing insect with sustenance.
Sweet box, *Sarcococca confusa*: A deliciously scented plant that is worth planting both for yourself and the insects.
Winter aconite, *Eranthis hyemalis*: Starts flowering in late winter, providing ample pollen for early emerging insects.
Hellebore/Christmas rose, *Helleborus*: Always flowers later than Christmas, but with big, beautiful flowers unlike anything else out in the depths of winter.

HELLEBORE

COMMON
IVY

SWEET
BOX

EVERGREEN
CLEMATIS

WINTER ACONITE

December

1 Start of meteorological winter

1 First Sunday in Advent (Christian)

13 St Lucia's Day (Christian)

21 Winter solstice, 09.19 — start of astronomical winter

21 Yule (Pagan midwinter celebration)

24 Christmas Eve (Christian)

25 Christmas Day (Christian) – bank holiday, England, Wales, Scotland, Northern Ireland and Ireland

25 Hanukkah – festival of lights (Jewish), begins at sundown

26 Boxing Day/St Stephen's Day (Christian), bank holiday England, Wales, Scotland, Northern Ireland, Ireland

31 New Year's Eve

DECEMBER IN THE GARDEN

The gardener, well wrapped, emerges from the busy, warm, brightly lit kitchen in a waft of spiced fruits and browning pastry scents, and heads with purpose to the end of the cold, quiet garden. The earth is dark and damp now, the stems bare, and boots on the path disturb nothing as the slumber is too deep. Creatures and plants alike have made their peace with the cold and the wet. They are pulled back into the earth or tucked under a duvet of soil or crumpled, softened leaf.

Only the robin might watch on, always nosy about events in what is now its territory, the gardener having temporarily withdrawn, save for the occasional foray outside to turn the steaming compost heap, or to push cloves of garlic into the earth – planted on the shortest day to harvest on the longest.

The gardener looks around, breath clouding, and then reaches up for the last remaining green, the evergreen, chosen as a reminder to those indoors that life still goes on out here in the solstice gloom, and that light will return. Branches of holly heavy with bright red berries prick at cold fingers, a crown of thorns to make a table centrepiece, bright with white candles and red ribbons. Arcs of ivy are gathered, to lay across mantelpieces and to twine up banisters. One task on an endless list ticked, the gardener retreats indoors.

The rest of the garden is left to the short and already dimming day, quickly turning to the long solstice night. There will be other plants chosen to join the warmth and light indoors later, but they await their moment, the Brussels sprouts standing lopsidedly, the parsnips lying under the earth.

And then, at this most unlikely moment of sleep and rest, when the garden is at its darkest, quietest and most abandoned, there is suddenly a change. A constellation of lights clicks on, white and shining, twinkling, draped over hedges and bare tree branches, and echoing the bright stars in the velvet winter sky above. A celebration of hope and new beginnings, at this darkest of moments, and of new life coming soon.

Garden and weather folklore

We now use the term 'halcyon days' to describe beautiful and endless summer days, but the original phrase referred to the dead of winter. Halcyon was the ancient Greek name for the kingfisher, and it was thought it calmed the winter seas, where it built a floating nest in which to lay its eggs. The phrase refers to a period of warm, settled weather around midwinter.

Any significant day in the year attracts weather folklore, and there is, of course, none more significant than Christmas Day. The old saying 'The nearer the new moon to Christmas Day, the harder the winter' doesn't bode well for us this year, with the new moon following just five days after Christmas Day. However, take heart because at Christmas: 'If the moon is bright and gleaming, next year's harvest will be poor. If the night is dark with no moon to be seen, harvest will be heavy and bountiful.'

Many of the pieces of Christmas weather lore follow a familiar pattern of 'if the weather is now like this, it will soon change to this' – for instance, 'At Christmas meadows green, at Easter covered with frost' or, more ominously, 'A green Christmas, a full churchyard'.

New Year's Eve, which is also St Sylvester's Day, is another significant day and an occasion to which much lore is attached. Winds are generally considered a bad sign:

> *'High winds on Sylvester's Day*
> *Will blow the New Year luck away.'*

However, the direction of the winds will also set the weather for the coming year:

> *'If New Year's Eve the wind blows South,*
> *It betokeneth warmth and growth*
> *If West, much milk and fish in the sea,*
> *If North, cold and storms there will be*
> *If East, the trees will bear much fruit,*
> *If North East, then flee it, man and brute.'*

D

THE SEA

Average sea temperature in Celcius

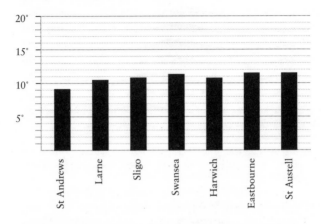

Spring and neap tides

Spring tides are the most extreme tides of the month, with the highest rises and the lowest falls, and they follow a couple of days after the full moon and new moon. These are the times to choose a low tide and go rock-pooling, mudlarking or coastal fossil-hunting. Neap tides are the least extreme, with the smallest movement, and they fall in between the spring tides.

Spring tides: 2nd–4th and 17th–19th

Neap tides: 8th–10th and 23rd–25th

Spring tides are shaded in black in the chart opposite.

December tide timetable for Dover

For guidance on how to convert this for your local area, see page 8.

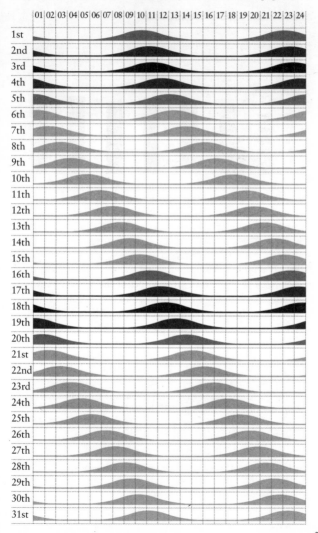

THE SKY

Stars, meteor showers and planets

Venus will appear as an evening star this month, becoming steadily more prominent thereafter. Look to the southwest in the early evening.

Jupiter is at opposition (its closest point to the earth, and highest and brightest) early in the month. Mars will be at its brightest and highest towards the end of the month. Saturn will also be visible in the evening hours.

4th: Brief early evening view of Venus and the crescent moon low in the southwest.

7th: Jupiter at opposition, and very bright all night long.

8th: Close approach of Saturn and the moon, rising together at dusk.

13th–14th: Geminid meteor shower. Visible from about 18.00 until 06.00 but an almost full moon means that only the brightest trails will be visible.

14th–17th: Close approach of Mars and the moon, rising together at dusk on the 14th, and then a little later each night (around 19.00 on 17th).

The sun

21st: Winter solstice. The winter solstice falls at 09.19. This is the moment that the sun is above the Tropic of Capricorn, the southernmost latitude that it can be directly overhead. The word solstice comes from the Latin *solstitium*, meaning 'sun standing still', and is related to the position of sunset and sunrise on the horizon. Both points have been heading south day by day and will now appear to pause a while, before setting off towards the north again.

21st: At solar noon the sun will reach an altitude of 15 degrees in the London sky and 11 degrees in the Glasgow sky.

Sunrise and set
Coton in the Elms, Derbyshire

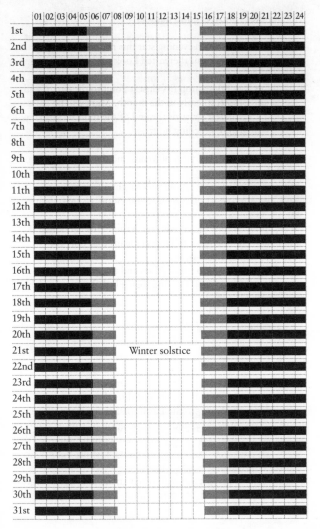

Moonrise and set

Like the sun, the moon rises roughly in the east and sets roughly in the west. It rises about 50 minutes later each day. Use the following guide to work out approximate moonrise times.

Full moon: Rises at around sunset time, but opposite the sun, so in the east as the sun sets in the west.
Last quarter: Rises at around midnight, and is at its highest point as the sun rises.
New moon: Rises at sunrise, in the same part of the sky as the sun, and so cannot be seen.
First quarter: Rises at around noon, and is at its highest point as the sun sets.

Moon phases

New moon – 1st December, 06.21

First quarter – 8th December, 15.27

Full moon – 15th December, 09.02

Last quarter – 22nd December, 22.18

New moon – 30th December, 22.27

The times given above are for the exact moment each moon phase occurs, for instance the moment that the moon is at its fullest.

December's full moon is known as the Oak Moon or Full Cold Moon. When it falls before midwinter, as it does this year, it is also the Moon Before Yule.

Moon phases for December

1st NEW	2nd	3rd	4th	5th
6th	7th	8th	9th	10th
11th	12th	13th	14th	15th FULL
16th	17th	18th	19th	20th
21st	22nd	23rd	24th	25th
26th	27th	28th	29th	30th NEW
31st				

MEDITATIONS

December's influences and guidance from Louise Press

Stillness cloaks the land as we enter December. Earth energy is strong under our feet. It draws down the life force of trees and plants, nourishing their roots and supporting their well-earned winter rest. The long hours of darkness encourage us, as human beings, to do the same. Winter is our natural rest-and-restore season. This time reminds us of the impermanence of life, the cycle of birth and death and the need to rest in order to rise. As the outer world surrenders its light, our inner world begins to sparkle and shine…there is healing going on inside.

The new moon in Sagittarius welcomes us into December on the 1st. There's nothing quite like an intentional start to the month. Sagittarius is full of big dreams and expansive ideas. So, in the quiet of deep winter, we can ride the energy of these moonbeams, be curious and gaze into our crystal ball to see with our mind's eye beyond the place we call home to adventures waiting in the wings for 2025.

The full moon in Gemini on 15th December arrives like a glitter ball to light up our dark December evenings. Aligned with the festive season, Gemini energy can be playful and extrovert. If you require wind beneath your wings to navigate the social scene, this full moon has the ability to transform you into a social butterfly with ease and grace.

We celebrate the winter solstice on 21st December, the darkest day of the year and the final 'in-breath' of the earth before the liminal moment of change as we tip into gentle expansion once again and step into Christmas.

Then, just as we think we're done for the year, December sneaks in a little gift…a second new moon is born on the 30th in Capricorn. We've been following the moon's guidance every month this year. We've dreamed into the year, put in the work, celebrated and harvested our achievements. We've recognised and let go of anything that hasn't worked for us, learned our lessons and evolved. This Capricorn new moon puts it all behind us and opens up the door to 2025, revealing exciting opportunities to do it all again.

Making a space for December

As all around are jingling bells, party dresses, sparkles and lights, make a nature table that connects you to what is going on outside, and to what this moment in the year is really all about. Use whites, reds and greens – for Christmas, yes, but also to remind you of the evergreens, those reassuring symbols of yule and the winter solstice, which we strew around our homes to remind us that not everything is dead.

Your table this month might include:
- Bare twigs and pine cones
- Evergreens, especially holly and ivy
- White candles, and white, red or green cloths
- A yule log
- Red and green ribbons
- Winter herbs – sage, rosemary and bay
- Pomander balls – oranges stuck with cloves and tied with ribbon
- A bowl of nuts and a nutcracker
- A glass of sherry and a mince pie (on Christmas Eve)

Light your candles all through this darkest of months, in the morning and the evening, adding found pieces from the outside world to your table as you come across them, and keeping that connection to outdoors even at this most indoor time. But make a special effort to take a moment to light the candles on the winter solstice, on the 21st, and to really take note of this moment that we have reached, the nadir of the year, after which the only way is up, lighter and brighter.

D

GARDENS

Gardening by the moon

The following is a guide to gardening with the phases of the moon, according to traditional practices. For moon-gardening cynics it also works as a guide to the month's gardening if you disregard the exact dates.

New moon to first quarter: 1st–8th December (until 15.27) and 31st December–6th January 2025
The waxing of the moon is associated with rising vitality and upward growth. Towards the end of this phase, plant and sow anything that develops crops above ground. Prepare for growth.
- Sow microgreens on a windowsill: basil, dill, celery, onion, chervil, beetroot, coriander, red mustard and pea. Harvest when 5cm tall.

First quarter to full moon: 8th (from 15.27)–14th December
This is the best time for sowing crops that develop above ground, but is bad for root crops. Take cuttings and make grafts but avoid all other pruning.
- Take grafts of favourite apple varieties to make new young plants.

Full moon to last quarter: 15th–22nd December
A 'drawing down' energy. This phase is a good time for sowing and planting any crops that develop below ground: root crops, bulbs and perennials.
- Prune grapevines before the winter solstice. The sap will start to rise very early in the new year and so they will 'bleed' if left any later.
- Plant garlic cloves.
- If the ground isn't frozen, plant new fruit bushes and trees.
- Plant rhubarb crowns. Lift, split and replant large clumps.
- Plant new perennials in your flower borders, and lift, divide and replant those that have finished flowering.

Last quarter to new moon: 23rd–30th December

A dormant period, with low sap and poor growth. Do not sow
or plant. A good time though for pruning, while sap is slowed.
Weeding now will check growth well. Harvest any crops for
storage. Mulch the soil. Garden maintenance.

- Prune apple, pear, medlar and quince trees.
- Check your soil's pH level. If it is low, below 6.5, now
  would be a good time to add lime or calcified seaweed. This
  raises the pH which in turn makes nutrients more easily
  available to plants. Brassicas in particular appreciate lime,
  but few vegetables grow well with a low pH.
- Mulch beds with organic manure.
- Weed thoroughly. This is a good time to get ahead with any
  perennial weed problems.
- Prune roses.
- Put terracotta pots onto 'pot feet' to lift them from the
  ground and improve drainage, ahead of the very cold
  months ahead.
- Protect any slightly tender plants and salad leaves from
  frost and winter weather by covering with horticultural
  fleece.
- Order seed for next year.

Note: Where no specific time for the change between phases is
mentioned, this is because it happens outside of usual
gardening hours. For exact changeover times for any late-night
or pre-dawn gardening, refer to the December moon phase
chart on page 268.

D

GARDEN CRAFT

Scandinavian straw stars

Traditional Scandinavian Christmas decorations are made of straw, tied in red thread, and you can make your own from garden stems and twigs. Cut lengths of a sturdy material, such as this year's young bamboo canes split into thin strips. If you are in the countryside, lengths of wheat straw would also be perfect.

You will need:
> 6 (or more) × 7cm lengths of sturdy material such as straw or split bamboo
> A board
> A drawing pin
> Red thread

To make a simple star, lay the straws flat on a board, crossing them all at the centre, like an asterisk. Pin the central point to the board with a drawing pin, and then space the straws evenly. Hold them in placing using the red threads, woven around the pin in the central point. Snip the ends of each straw diagonally, so that they are all the same length. Pierce one end of one straw and thread a loop through it to hang the ornament from the tree.

   If you have more straws, you can make this design more complicated by tying a straw between the points of every third star, to make first a triangle, and then a six-pointed star; or try other patterns, such as linking every other straw. To make it pretty and sturdy, tie red thread wherever straws meet.

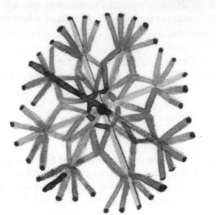

NATURE

Garden wildlife in December

In winter the soil can freeze down to a maximum of about 45cm, a depth known as the frost line. Before this happens, earthworms burrow down into the subsoil, rolling into a tight ball and covering themselves with a protective layer of mucus, enabling them to survive without moisture. Amphibians also bury themselves in the soil or tuck themselves beneath stones and logs. Some frogs, particularly males, overwinter at the bottom of ponds, breathing though their skin. In freezing conditions, a frog stops breathing and its heart stops beating – it survives thanks to high levels of glucose in its vital organs. It will thaw out and resume life as soon as temperatures increase.

Some invertebrates, such as springtails, can also survive being frozen for a short period of time, and will simply defrost as temperatures increase again. Bacteria, too, can survive being frozen without injury. Some soil microorganisms remain active, although at a much slower pace. And, while many species of soil fungi don't actively survive winter, setting spores instead, mycorrhizal fungi (see page 140) can remain active, surviving within the root tissues of host plants.

Like soil fauna, perennial plants and trees have evolved to survive freezing conditions. Most plants that evolved to grow in colder climates develop root systems below the frost layer. Freezing can cause root cells to rupture, effectively killing the plant, and so they have nifty ways to prevent it. Plant root cells contain higher concentrations of sugars and salts, which lower the freezing point of water inside them, effectively working as an antifreeze. Roots can also release water into the surrounding soil, minimising damage caused by freezing temperatures.

The healthiest soils play the greatest role in insulating soil fauna and plant roots against the cold. Organic matter, such as leaves and other plant material, as well as mulches of materials like leaf mould or compost, holds on to heat below ground. It won't be long before it all warms up again though, ready for a whole new year of life.

THE KITCHEN

Cooking from the garden in December

Here are some crops that you might find in the kitchen garden this month: beetroot, Brussels sprouts, cabbages, carrots, cauliflowers, celeriac, celery, chard, chicory, garlic, kale, leeks, lettuces, onions, Oriental leaves, spring onions, parsnips, potatoes, pumpkins, winter squashes, spinach, swedes, turnips, chervil, parsley, coriander, sage, rosemary, bay, pears, apples.

Ideas for eating from the garden this month

- Bubble and squeak topped with a runny fried egg.
- Coleslaw made with shredded sprouts, grated carrots, thin batons of apple and a handful of toasted pumpkin and sesame seeds.
- Parsnips roasted in maple syrup to eat with slices of ham.
- Curry of spinach, potatoes, onions, garam masala, turmeric, ginger and a finishing dash of cream, with chapatis or boiled rice.
- Nutmeg-heavy baked rice pudding served with a dollop of apple sauce and chopped toasted pecans.

SNACK OF THE MONTH

Sgagliozze (fried polenta)

Fourth-century St Nicholas (known as *Sinterklaas* in Dutch) was the model for Santa Claus, who evolved from *Sinterklaas* traditions and originated in the saint's habit of secret gift giving, as well as his penchant for dropping sacks of gold coins down the chimneys of the needy. His feast day, 6th December, is celebrated in many European countries with gifts for children. His relics were interred at Basilica di San Nicola in Bari, Italy, and special services are held there on the 6th. But more importantly for our purposes, he also has his own very delicious snack, *sgagliozze*, fried pieces of polenta flavoured with herbs, which are sold outside the cathedral on the big day.

Makes about 16 pieces

2 tablespoons good-quality olive oil, plus extra for frying and greasing

1 tablespoon salt

100g polenta

½ teaspoon ground cinnamon

½ teaspoon ground black pepper

small spring of rosemary, finely chopped

a few leaves of sage, finely chopped

Method

Grease a 23 × 35cm baking tray. Bring 450ml water to the boil, then reduce the heat to a simmer and add the salt. Add the polenta in a slow stream, whisking continuously to avoid lumps. The polenta will thicken quite quickly, and beware of volcanically hot bubbles spluttering out of the pan. Continue to whisk over a low heat for a minute or so, until the mixture comes away from the sides of the pan and gives a little resistance against the whisk. Stir in the olive oil, cinnamon, pepper and herbs. Taste and add extra seasoning if needed; it needs more salt than you might imagine. Using a spatula or the back of a spoon, smooth the polenta out over the greased baking tray and allow it to cool completely.

When cool, slice it into squares or triangles. Pour olive oil into a frying pan to a depth of about 5mm and heat it until medium hot. Place a few pieces of polenta in the pan, being careful not to overcrowd it. Cook for a few minutes on one side, avoiding the temptation to turn them too soon. You don't want to flip these back and forth, as they may fall apart and not be as crispy. After a few minutes, turn to crisp up the other side, then lift out onto a plate lined with kitchen paper. Repeat with the rest of the polenta. Allow to cool slightly before eating on their own or with a simple dip of puréed sundried tomatoes.

D

FOLK SONG

'Cherry Tree Carol'
Traditional, arr. Richard Barnard

A very old song known to have been sung since at least the 15th century. Mary and Joseph are travelling to Bethlehem when they pass a cherry orchard and Mary asks Joseph to gather some cherries for her. When he refuses – 'Let him gather thee cherries that got thee with child' – Jesus pipes up from the womb, and makes sure Mary gets her cherries before a chastened Joseph. There are many variations and this tune is closest to a traditional Cornish version.

O, Joseph was an old man,
And an old man was he,
And Joseph married Mary,
The Queen of Galilee.

So Joseph and Mary
Through a garden did go,
Where cherries a-plenty
On every tree did grow.

O, then bespoke Mary
With words meek and mild,
'O, gather me cherries,
For I am with child.'

And then replied Joseph
with words so unkind,
'Let him gather thee cherries
That got thee with child.'

O, then bespoke our Saviour
In his mother's womb,
'Bow down, good cherry tree
For to give my mother some.'

The uppermost sprig
It bowed down to Mary's knee,
'Thus you may see, Joseph,
These cherries are for me.'

D

FURTHER INFORMATION

'Lia's Living Almanac' is my free weekly newsletter all about the turning of the year. It has developed into a community of like-minded people coming together to notice and mark the seasons. Join us at lialeendertz.substack.com

Foods of England Project is a fabulous resource of old traditional English recipes and the stories behind them. It was the inspiration for my take on plum shuttles for Valentine's Day. www.foodsofengland. co.uk

The Bumblebee Flies Anyway – a Year of Gardening and (Wild) Life by Almanac nature contributor Kate Bradbury

The Joy of Snacks by Laura Goodman, for more ideas on delicious snacks to nibble

Telling the Seasons by Martin Maudsley – a beautiful and informative new book about celebrations and folklore around the year

REFERENCES

Astronomical and calendrical information reproduced with
    permission from HM Nautical Almanac Office (HMNAO), UK
    Hydrographic Office (UKHO) and the Controller of Her
    Majesty's Stationery Office.
Moon and sun rises and sets and further calculations reproduced with
    permission from www.timeanddate.com
Tidal predictions reproduced with permission from HMNAO, UKHO
    and the Controller of Her Majesty's Stationery Office.
Astronomical events are based on ephemerides obtained using the
    NASA JPL Horizons system.
Sea temperatures are reproduced with permission from
    www.seatemperature.org.

INDEX

ACKNOWLEDGEMENTS

This edition has had more contributors than ever before. Thanks to everyone who has played a part in creating the 2024 almanac – it has been a joy curating such a talented bunch.

It was wonderful to have frog aficionado Kate Bradbury (Twitter: @Kate_Bradbury) on board to write the nature sections this year, as nerdy as they are poetic. Thank you.

Thank you to Louise Press (Instagram: @onewomanawake) for beautiful work on the sections on the guidance of the moon phases, bringing a slice of her magical yurt to my almanac. I am thrilled to have you on board.

Thank you to composer Richard Barnard (website: RichardBarnard. com) for researching and putting together the folk songs in this edition. As ever your care and creativity are hugely appreciated.

Thanks to Beth Al-Rikabi (website: beththefreerangechef.com) again for such creative and thorough help on recipe development and testing.

Thanks to my dad, Jack Leendertz, for ever-diligent work on the sky at night sections.

Zara Chang sent me her gorgeous seasonal poetry, which I didn't use in the end, but which sparked some of the thoughts in the chapter introductions and from which I have used a few lines, with permission. Thank you, Zara.

I am so delighted to have been able to work with illustrator Aitch, having admired her work for years. It feels like the perfect fit, thank you.

Thanks to almanac designer Matt Cox of Newman+Eastwood for turning the book out so beautifully each year. And to everyone at Octopus Publishing and Gaia, thank you so much for taking such care over it: Stephanie Jackson, Jonathan Christie, Pauline Bache, Marianne Laidlaw, Matt Grindon, Hazel O'Brien, Rosa Patel, Pete Hunt, Alison Wormleighton, Laura Gladwin and Claudia Connal.

Thanks also to my agent, Adrian Sington at Kruger Cowne Ltd, for your guidance and support.

And finally, love and thanks to my gorgeous family.